"In a market saturated with daunting technological treatises on new media, Lena Claxton and Alison Woo have written a clear, concise, step-by-step manual that offers plenty of truly useful tips yet never feels confusing. The authors don't just tell us what to do to succeed on the Internet, they show us how to do it."

　　—Marie-France Han, reporter for Reuters

"This book is a must-read for every business owner who wants to harness the power of the Internet. Its groundbreaking premise of integrating all the elements of new media, plus guiding business owners on what to say, is sure to propel your business to new levels of success."

　　—Michelle Anton, author of *Weekend Entrepreneur*,

　　　http://weekend.entrepreneur.com

"The perfect book for first-time or experienced marketing people who want new media information explained easily and completely. Lena Claxton and Alison Woo are two savvy pros who have written a how-to book on new media marketing that explains everything you need to know in easy terms so you'll never feel confused."

　　—Kate Bacon, blogger for Broadcasting & Cable and WellDunne PR

"With the technology advances driving my industry, it's crucial to have a guide through the wilderness. Whether it's building a user-friendly website or utilizing e-zines to extend your company's brand, the authors weave together the elements you need to meet the demands of today's marketplace."

　　—Fredda Sacharow, former editorial page editor,

　　　Burlington (NJ) County Times

continued...

"As someone in charge of helping small business owners at one of the largest chambers of commerce in the nation, I found this book to be the quintessential guide for any business that wishes to maximize the full potential of the web to connect authentically and to bring value to its customers."

—Steven Partridge, senior vice president of Member Value,
Charlotte Chamber of Commerce

"From cover to cover this book is informative, enlightening, and inspiring! Entrepreneurs and aspiring business owners will be hard-pressed to find another resource that provides guidance and direction on small business promotion as *How to Say It: Marketing with New Media*. I would encourage anyone interested in truly moving their business into the twenty-first century to pick up a copy today and tell a friend!"

—Edward Foxworth III, author of *It's Just Domino's*

"Lena Claxton and Alison Woo take the diverse and varied elements that get grouped together as 'new media' and present them in an organized and manageable format that will be of great value for small business entrepreneurs. Had their book been available when we launched the Hall Institute in 2005, it would have helped us build our public presence more quickly and more efficiently."

—Richard A. Lee, communications director of
Hall Institute of Public Policy

"After reading *How to Say It: Marketing with New Media*, I feel like the cavemen must have felt the day they discovered fire. No more rubbing sticks together or hoping lightning will strike! Thanks to Lena Claxton and Alison Woo, I now have the tools I need to market my own business and those of my clients. I'm leaving old-fashioned press releases and media kits back in the cave and moving quickly and decidedly into twenty-first-century marketing—with this insightful and exceedingly helpful book as my guide."

—Rex John, founder/owner of
Rex John & Associates Public Relations

"This smart, savvy, and user-friendly guide provides readers with the simple ins and outs of digital marketing. Straightforward and practical, this is the guide that all small business owners need to roll up their sleeves and start using the Internet as a powerful tool to reach out, connect with customers, and drive sales."

—Angela Kyle, media entrepreneur and
co-creator of www.virginsguide.com

"The book is excellent! The authors really do a great job. It is very insightful and educational. Learning to conduct business through Internet resources is very complicated to most and can be confusing to say the least. This book provides great insight to the various areas that can be utilized and great detail on how to go about doing it. I learned a lot from the information provided. This is a very educational step-by-step guide on utilizing the Internet to create a successful business."

—Lori Thames, MBA; division director of
Boswell Regional Center

"Claxton and Woo have compiled an indispensable reference for any small business new to web 2.0. Comprehensive discussions of e-zines, blogs, and podcasts provide invaluable insights on everything from customer engagement to RSS feeds to search engine optimization. *How to Say It: Marketing with New Media* is loaded with industry-specific examples of how to leverage the opportunities presented by the new web landscape, and consistently strikes a balance between illuminating the art and technology behind a successful web marketing campaign. Read this book, follow the directions, and unlock the full potential of your business."

—Thomas Fishman, head of online productions
at ScienCentral, Inc.

"This is a must-have for any business owner. Large or small, all businesses would benefit by the knowledge and information given to us on these pages."

—John R. Carney, program director of Contracted Training,
Kirkwood Community College

continued...

"This book will inspire even serious 'non-techies' to jump on the new media bandwagon. The comprehensive content gives you the step-by-step on how to use popular online tools to effectively communicate with customers—all in an easy-to-read format written in everyday language. Most helpful are the industry-specific tips throughout the book, as well as suggested services to handle everything you need to get started with new media today!"

  —Barbara Hall, director of Small Business Center,
   Rowan-Cabarrus Community College

"*How to Say It: Marketing with New Media* is an indispensable and easy-to-understand guide to marketing using the latest online tools. If you are serious about promoting your business, you must take advantage of the web and 'new media.' With billions of people using the Internet, business owners must take advantage of the low-cost global marketing platform the World Wide Web has to offer. This guide is the perfect first step to becoming web savvy—its step-by-step guidance will make you a new media–marketing pro! Simply put, this is a must-have book for small business owners seeking to succeed in today's highly competitive web-driven business world."

  —Renee Hode, director of Institute of Entrepreneurship,
   Central Piedmont Community College

"Lena and Alison's book includes a buffet of new, evolving IT media business practices, tools, and methods. I learned many new IT updates in Internet media by reading their book. Some of the most notable are e-zines, RentACoder.com, and Yooter."

  —John Martinez, BSIT, information technology professional

"Every question you ever had about doing business online—answered!"

  —Colleen Moriarty, author of *Shortcuts to Sexy Abs*

HOW TO SAY IT
Marketing with New Media

A Guide to Promoting Your Small Business
Using Websites, E-zines, Blogs, and Podcasts

LENA CLAXTON and ALISON WOO

Prentice Hall Press

PRENTICE HALL PRESS
Published by the Penguin Group
Penguin Group (USA) Inc.
375 Hudson Street, New York, New York 10014, USA
Penguin Group (Canada), 90 Eglinton Avenue East, Suite 700, Toronto, Ontario M4P 2Y3, Canada
(a division of Pearson Penguin Canada Inc.)
Penguin Books Ltd., 80 Strand, London WC2R 0RL, England
Penguin Group Ireland, 25 St. Stephen's Green, Dublin 2, Ireland (a division of Penguin Books Ltd.)
Penguin Group (Australia), 250 Camberwell Road, Camberwell, Victoria 3124, Australia
(a division of Pearson Australia Group Pty. Ltd.)
Penguin Books India Pvt. Ltd., 11 Community Centre, Panchsheel Park, New Delhi—110 017, India
Penguin Group (NZ), 67 Apollo Drive, Rosedale, North Shore 0632, New Zealand
(a division of Pearson New Zealand Ltd.)
Penguin Books (South Africa) (Pty.) Ltd., 24 Sturdee Avenue, Rosebank, Johannesburg 2196, South Africa

Penguin Books Ltd., Registered Offices: 80 Strand, London WC2R 0RL, England

While the author has made every effort to provide accurate telephone numbers and Internet addresses at the time of publication, neither the publisher nor the author assumes any responsibility for errors, or for changes that occur after publication. Further, the publisher does not have any control over and does not assume any responsibility for author or third-party websites or their content.

First edition: September 2008

Library of Congress Cataloging-in-Publication Data

Claxton, Lena.
  How to say it : marketing with new media : a guide to promoting your small business
using websites, e-zines, blogs, and podcasts / Lena Claxton and Alison Woo.
    p.   cm.
  Includes bibliographical references and index.
  ISBN 978-0-7352-0432-4
  1. Internet marketing.   2. Small business—Computer networks.   3. Website development.
4. Internet advertising.   I. Woo, Alison.   II. Title.
  HF5415.1265.C578   2008
  658.8'72—dc22   2008015858

PRINTED IN THE UNITED STATES OF AMERICA

10   9   8   7   6   5   4

Most Prentice Hall Press books are available at special quantity discounts for bulk purchases for sales promotions, premiums, fund-raising, or educational use. Special books, or book excerpts, can also be created to fit specific needs. For details, write: Special Markets, Penguin Group (USA) Inc., 375 Hudson Street, New York, New York 10014.

This book is for all who summon the entrepreneurial spirit to explore new frontiers.

ACKNOWLEDGMENTS

Nothing in life happens in a vacuum. The amount of support and encouragement needed to create anything is both humbling and life affirming. This book would never have been a reality if it weren't for Sarah Jane Freymann and Jessica Sinsheimer of the Sarah Jane Literary Agency, who discovered, nurtured, and advocated for the project; and special thanks to Maria Gagliano, our editor at Penguin/Prentice Hall Press, who saw the potential in our idea, nourished it, and made it even better. We are forever grateful to Candace Levy, our copyeditor extraordinaire, and the entire production and sales teams at Penguin, who laid these pages out, designed a smashing cover, and made this book available around the world.

Thank you to our New Media Mavens clients who were so supportive of this material when we launched our seminars, which inspired us to write this book.

Lena: Thanks to Alison, my friend and coauthor whose positive energy is contagious! Thanks to my supportive friends—they know who they are. My siblings, Cissy, Thelma, Bev, and Doug, are my rock! To Mom and Dad: Hermine and Walpole Rose, also Victor Rose and Margurite Claxton—I treasure you forever. To my husband, John, for his love and unwavering support. To my son Andre for his support and his out-of-the-box thinking. To my son Marc for his creativity and lovely spirit.

Alison: To my dear friend and colleague Lena: I've enjoyed every minute of our adventure. You are an inspiration! Thank you to all of my extraordinary friends—including Doggie, Kat, Kay, Kate, Trish, Regan, Carline, Nancy, Tony, Sandra, and Sandy—who always encourage me to stretch beyond my limits. My deepest gratitude goes to my "godmother" Johanna, who opened the door to a much greater world. But most of all, my heartfelt thanks to my family—Vera, Joe, and Michael Woo (my mom, dad, and brother), who steadfastly believe that "anyone born the year man walked on the moon can achieve anything."

CONTENTS

Part Three:
Getting Your Message Across ... With an E-zine

Part Four:
Getting Your Message Across ... With a Blog

Part Five:
Getting Your Message Across…With a Podcast

Part Six:
Putting It All Together

FOREWORD

Technology's most important role is to connect people to one another. "The more you think about business as being a community service, the more successful you become," said Craig Newmark, founder of CraigsList.

When I started eWomen Network in the garage over my Dallas home, it began with the mission of connecting the incredible entrepreneurs I was meeting and helping them create a place where they could have their own community. Our initial goal was to be high-tech, but soon we became high-touch. As entrepreneurs made powerful connections online, they wanted to meet each other face to face. Now, several years later, as the founder and CEO of eWomen Network, I'm proud to say that our website is the most-visited women's business site on the World Wide Web, receiving more than 300,000 hits daily. Our site brings together entrepreneurs who are passionate about their business and who end up doing business with one another. It has even spawned more than sixty-five local chapters, in which entrepreneurs connect monthly to network and do business together. Building community is certainly the future of business communication.

In today's marketplace, communicating with your customers is the single most important thing a business can do. For businesses, this is not about surviving; it's about thriving. Customers and clients are savvy: They want comprehensive information on their schedule. Businesses that use new media applications, such as blogs, e-zines, podcasts, and websites, are poised to provide their existing and future customers with essential information. This information could relate to how to solve a problem, connect them with information or a resource they need to know about, or it could be information that is enlightening or entertaining. The goal for businesses should be to become indispensable.

This book, *How to Say It: Marketing with New Media: A Guide to Promoting Your Small Business Using Websites, E-zines, Blogs, and Podcasts*, equips small business owners with all the tools they will need to communicate with prospects and customers around the corner and around the globe.

This is not another technical manual. It incorporates a fresh approach that guides the business owner in exactly how to speak and connect with his or her audience. It is a marketing and communication resource that will certainly take your business to the next level.

As the title suggests, the content is focused on four distinct areas of new media technologies: websites, e-zines, blogs, and podcasts. But the authors don't just leave you to apply these applications randomly; they offer communication strategies that you can use in your business now. You will know not only how to find your target audience for these technologies but how to put it all together so that you have a powerful, integrated marketing system.

It is my privilege to wholeheartedly recommend this helpful book to all small business owners who want to harness the power of the Internet to spread the word about their business and build their own successful community.

—Sandra Yancey

Sandra Yancey is founder and CEO of eWomen Network, Inc. (www.ewomen network.com) and is the author of the book *Relationship Networking: The Art of Turning Contacts into Connections*. Her story is featured in *Chicken Soup for the Entrepreneur's Soul*.

Part One

Setting the Stage for New Media Success

ONE

WHAT CAN NEW MEDIA DO FOR YOUR BUSINESS?

Marketing with new media will revolutionize the way you do business.

In today's marketplace, you have to grab customers' attention quickly with succinct website content, create e-zines that will keep them engaged, interact regularly through your blog, and keep them listening to your podcasts. New media equips you to earn and keep your customers' interest, their business, and much more. But despite new media's numerous benefits, not everyone is on board. According to a 2007 Jupiter Research survey, only 36 percent of all businesses with fewer than 100 employees had a web presence.[1] If you are one of these business owners, this book will help strengthen your online presence. If you are embarking on your business or your new media pursuits, this book will equip you to start off strong.

Tapping into the power of new media is not about just having a flashy website. The true value lies in *what you say*. When used effectively, these communication tools will help you build a community of loyal customers that you can connect with at any time. You cannot afford to be left behind.

Marketing with new media gives you the biggest bang for your buck—both in time and in money. It allows you to talk to millions with the ease of talking to one; it gives you control over how, when, and where you talk to your

Some of the examples throughout this book come from real websites. You will find their URLs provided in these cases. Many of the samples were created from our years of experience consulting with small businesses. Most of the examples featured in this book are geared toward the top small business categories as provided by the Internal Revenue Service:

Construction	Manufacturing
Retail trade	Real estate
Professional, scientific, and technical services	Finance and insurance
	Religious
Healthcare and social assistance	Educational services
Accommodations and food service	Writers and performing artists
Wholesale trade	
Administrative, support, and waste management	

customers and how they talk to you; and it gives you a built-in fan base—the lifeblood of your thriving business.

This book will empower you to use the right tools, at the right time, in the right context and will show you how to speak to the right audience.

Using new media allows for a deep and potentially rewarding way to shift and expand your business mind-set. The bottom line is that you want to boost business. But just about anyone can get a professional-looking website, rant on a blog, send e-zines, or post podcasts. Just how you use these powerful new media tools is what will set you apart from your competition. You cannot use a cookie-cutter approach. The days of the one-size-fits-all business model are over.

If you want to revitalize your marketing efforts, we encourage you to take a holistic approach: Apply the tenets of *organic small business.*

The organic movement was initially concerned with what we put into

Three Tenets of Organic Small Business

Truth. You must be true to yourself.

Value. What you offer must make a difference to your customer or client.

Commitment. You must make a commitment to be part of your community for the long haul.

our bodies. It evolved into what we put into our environment. As New Media Mavens, we have taken this idea to the next step. It's now about what we, as a society, put of ourselves into our businesses and our communities.

As marketing and new media experts, we have helped businesses transcend to a new level, from the old ways of business as usual to the incorporation of the ideals of organic small business. This allows for more passion, more fulfillment, and attracts the kinds of customers that you want.

This is a revolutionary way of approaching your entire business and means that your marketing should not be separate from your business philosophy. Owning an organic small business encourages you to take the core essentials of who you are and apply them to your work. Within each "Core Essentials" section of this book, you'll learn how to put your authentic stamp on each new media component. In the end, it is your uniqueness that will help you stand out from the crowd.

All of the new media channels—websites, e-zines, blogs, and podcasts—encourage a fresh approach to doing business that is actually hinged on an old-fashioned mind-set. It's amazing that the advent of new technology can take us back to the old way of doing business. We're going back to the roots of our customer relationships—being heart centered. We're going back to cultivating grassroots businesses.

Back in the day of mom-and-pop businesses, you would build relationships one customer at a time, within your town. When customers walked into your store or business, you spoke to them individually, shook their hands, looked into their eyes, listened to them, and serviced their needs. It was a win–win situation, in which you felt good and the customer felt good.

Today, new media allows you to replicate this model online and achieve the same results on a much larger scale. Imagine, a prospect drops by your blog and your topic strikes a chord with him. He leaves a comment. You respond. Others drop by and leave their comments. Others respond. Before you know it, you have a conversation going. More than likely your contacts download one or two freebies that you offer and sign up for your mailing list. You can continue this and other conversations forever. Your one message, the topic you posted online, reached not one or two people, but hundreds or more. These individuals could live next door or on the other side of the world, it doesn't matter. Your message is just as timely and fresh.

This approach to doing business is built for long-term sustainability, not just short-term profits. It means approaching your business holistically and looking at the imprint your business makes. It encourages authentic, open conversations between the business owner and the customer without the artifice of slick advertising or a middle man telling you what to buy and when. You're going to talk to your customer directly, honestly, with his or her best benefit in mind. It's about speaking from your heart to your customer's heart. It means creating businesses that focus on service, not sales, knowing that if you fulfill a customer's need, the sales will always follow. It's not just one sale you are looking for; it is years of future sales and lasting relationships.

Using new media allows you to drop the veil and be more accessible and personal. In all of your communications with your customer you will always speak directly to your customer's needs, pain, and challenges.

It's about Time

One of the biggest challenges you face as a business owner is figuring out how to do more in less time. It's also an issue that affects your customers, who can barely take the time to hear what you have to say.

Automation makes repetitive actions easy—like reminding customers about upcoming sales. You can spend one day every six months scheduling all of your e-mail blasts promoting your events. If you don't like blogging daily, you can sit down for one hour a week and set your posts to hit your blog on specified days. Or if you fear you'll waste valuable minutes trying to decide what to write about in your e-zine, this book will show you how to create a formula that will keep you on track month after month, year after year. The time you save will give you the time to create snazzy, compelling content.

Technology allows you to connect directly with your customer; but to some degree, this opportunity is a double-edged sword. A 2008 National Workplace Productivity Survey, sponsored by LexisNexis, asked professionals in twenty-three different sectors how they process information in their jobs.[2] Seventy-three percent of those surveyed said they were overloaded with information. In the same study, 62 percent of those surveyed said they filter through irrelevant information. Web users are inundated with MTV-style messages that are fast and slick, and that contribute to this massive information overload. Add that to our decreasing attention spans, and the result is a generation of consumers who demand succinct messages that cut through the clutter.

The new media tools we offer in this book will help your business and your message stand out from the noise. For each of the tools we recommend, we'll show you how to speak to your always-evolving audience, who are becoming more savvy, edgier, and more impatient every day.

It's about What You Say and How You Say It

While websites, e-zines, blogs, and podcasts are the vehicles you use for communicating, it's what you say that matters most. What you say and how you say it directly affects how your customers relate to you. Successful interactions happen when your words about your product or service connect with the needs or desires of your customer.

This book is designed to help you choose precisely the right words and phrases to create the environment in which your customer feels valued and part of the relationship. Today's customer has been bombarded by sales talk a million times over. It is not about browbeating your customer into submission. What this book offers are the words that initiate a dialogue with your customers. It also shows you how to use language in a new way to help create and cement long-lasting relationships.

It's about Creating Community

New media multiplies your relationships so that you can build your own community. You start by fostering a relationship based on two-way communication, in which the customer, not you, is at the heart of your communication. Your community sees your business as indispensable in meeting its needs and wants.

Building an online community is the single most important thing you can do to grow your business. A community is a group of people who are your most loyal customers—a network of consumers who consistently want what you have to offer. These are the people who refer your business to others. These are the same consumers you will focus your marketing efforts on over and over. Yes, the old axiom of people doing business with whom they know, like, and trust is as true now as it was in the past.

Creating your online community also provides your business with an informal focus group, informing you about the innovations your customers need or want. For example, a homebuilder can send a survey with questions such as, *What upgrades would you like to see in your next home?* A fitness center could ask, *What fitness challenges would you like to conquer?* You'll get fast feedback that helps you tailor your business offerings to what your customers want. In traditional marketing, businesses pay tens of thousands of dollars to get research from focus groups. New media allows for a much more cost-effective, honest approach.

New media tools help you build an online community with ease. According to a Pew Internet Study, "people exchange e-mails, hash out issues, find out about group activities, and meet face-to-face as a result of online communities. Approximately 23 million Americans are very active in online communities, meaning that they e-mail their principal online group several times a week."

Some of the most appealing features for customers include business responsiveness and a place that offers support and creates affinity with other community members. Virtual, or online, communities also rely on user-generated content and open forums, allowing communication without censorship. The anonymity factor allows your customers to be more truthful, which helps you hear what they actually like or dislike about your product or service.

No doubt, new media helps you build a successful community. You can have the fanciest site, a constantly updated blog, an informative e-zine, and frequent podcasts; but if you do not have a customer base—a target audience—your efforts will be in vain.

The ultimate goal of business owners is to carve out a community from the vast pool of their target audience. For example, let's say you offer women's narrow-width shoes to a universe of women shoe buyers. New media allows for a faster, wider, and deeper penetration of this market than traditional marketing techniques. By inviting potential customers to comment on your blog, asking them to send in questions about their challenges to your e-zine, encouraging them to download your podcasts about the latest fall shoe fashions, or holding a contest on your website, you begin to shape that large target audience into an engaging, interactive community.

What New Media Cannot Do

New media cannot replace face-to-face communication. Technology is a supplement, not a replacement, for human contact. New media serves to enhance that conversation.

New media cannot reach your entire customer base. Not everyone has joined the digital world, so you need to continue with traditional marketing. All your print marketing materials, such as business cards, postcards, newsletters, and brochures should have your website information, including your website address (URL), your e-mail address, and your blog address (URL).

New media cannot provide instant gratification. Like any other aspect of your business, creating a new media platform is a process. It's not a silver bullet. Consistent efforts will make a significant difference.

TWO

FINDING YOUR TARGET AUDIENCE

How to Find Your Target Audience

You already know the product or service that you want to offer, so the next step is to find a receptive audience. A target audience is the group of people who use and want your products or services. Your audience can stem from specific geographic areas, a specialty industry, or a specific demographic such as an ethnic group or population that may be overlooked or has a need that is not already being served by others.

When you serve a core group or target audience online, several things need to happen. You need to (1) *speak* specifically and directly to your audience, not just to any arbitrary person who may be surfing the web, (2) *express* yourself with authority on your audience's needs, becoming the go-to person and expert in your field, and (3) *connect* with your audience by offering valuable information.

Redefine Your Audience

Just as with traditional marketing principles, even if you already have a general idea of who you want to do business with, it's a good idea to redefine your target market periodically, especially if sales are languishing (but ideally *before* they do). Redefining can be as simple as reframing what you already do. A classic example is Domino's Pizza. They took ordinary pizza and targeted it to people who want it fast—in thirty minutes or less. Blockbuster took a video rental service and made it "a night in," targeting people who'd rather enjoy movies in the comfort of their own homes than go to the theater.

From these *reframes*, we see a laser focus on specific audiences—the target audiences of those businesses. To be effective, every message communicated to the target audience has to resonate, serve its specialized needs, and have an emphasis on building community. Some ways of inspiring community are e-mail coupons, website polls, and contests for naming new products or items.

Know Who You Are and Who You Aren't

Before you can identify your ideal customer, you need to know who you are. Consider this African folk tale: A mouse and a sausage befriended each other and used to scavenge for bits of lettuce and vegetables to make soup. The sausage, in charge of cooking, used to jump in the pot just before the soup was done to give the broth some flavor. The mouse, grateful for all the sausage had done, thought that he would take over the cooking duties for a change and make dinner. Just before the soup was done, the mouse jumped in—and died.

The moral of the story: Know who you are and who you aren't. In your business, focus on a core audience that you want to work with and that is aligned with the mission of your business. Avoid groups and markets that don't feel right—you will not be attuned to their needs. If patience is not your virtue, don't offer chartered bus services to the handicapped. Avoid opening a Mexican restaurant when you enjoy Italian food best.

If your business feels stagnant and you're not connecting with your customers, if you feel drained every day and work has become a chore, now is the time to reevaluate and make a fundamental shift. Get clear on what precisely you are unhappy about. Envision the type of work that you would find fulfilling. This process can be as subtle as shifting your own mind-set and how you show up mentally, physically, emotionally, and spiritually at work. It could lead to introducing new programs or extending your brand into creating another product line or service. It could also be attracting different kinds of customers.

If you're a bit unclear or unable to determine the group you want to work with, you may want to explore the following broad-based questions: (1) Who has a problem I can solve with my expertise? (2) With whom do I like to work? (3) Is this group easy to reach? (4) Is this group able to pay me for my services or products? (f) Is this group large enough to sustain my business?

Questions to Refine Your Target Audience Profile

Once you've determined the big picture of exactly who makes up your target audience—restaurants, churches, corporations, authors, salespeople, home-based businesses, lawyers, crafters, stay-at-home parents, musicians, artists, athletes, students, travelers, home buyers, accountants, financial planners, dentists, executives, consultants, therapists—the next step is to fine-tune the details and dig even deeper. Some questions to consider include the following:

Where does your audience live?
What is the average monthly income of your audience?
Is your audience made up of men, women, or both?
How old is your audience?
What are your audience's interests?
What kind of books or magazines does your audience read?
What does your audience watch?
What does your audience listen to?
What does your audience buy?

The answers to these questions will help you create a composite of your ideal customer. These answers will directly affect where and how you'll market to *your* audience and what you will say to it.

Building an organic small business allows you to make decisions that honor your core beliefs and express your authenticity. It starts with choosing who you want to work with. Before you commit to working with one target audience, you may want to consider a couple of potential target audiences to see how you actually feel about working with each of the groups you've chosen.

Focus on one of the groups you identified in "Questions to Refine Your Target Audience Profile" (page 13). Live with your choice for a few minutes in your mind. Pay close attention to the way you feel. Do you feel excited by the idea of working with this group? Or do you get a sinking feeling? Avoid succumbing to other motives such as wanting to target a group or area of industry solely because of money. Although in the short run focusing on that target audience may provide an influx of cash, organic small business practitioners measure success using a wide range of indicators, including long-term fulfillment and passion not just profits.

Once you have a composite of your ideal customer, complete another profile for other potential groups within your audience, for example, couples or seniors. Continue testing your feelings with a third and fourth set of target customers and notice which groups raise your positive vibrations. Remember: If it feels good, it is good.

As a result of pinpointing who you are and who you aren't, you will gain a desire to interact on a deeper level with your audience. Once you've tapped into the target audience that you have the most natural affinity with, your passion will propel you to interact naturally. You'll find yourself talking to people based on a true desire to find out what they're thinking and what they're up to.

Essentials of Speaking to the Right Audience

Once you evaluate and select your target audience, the next step is to formulate a marketing message to clearly communicate what you offer. Before you write one word on your website, blog, or e-zine or speak on your podcast, make sure your content directly addresses your selected group and consistently aims to attract the prospects you want.

Creating Your Marketing Message

A marketing message is a succinct statement that explains the purpose of your business to your target audience. It is no coincidence that the marketing message has been nicknamed the "elevator speech." You should be able to say what you do, who you do it for, and the benefits you provide in the time it takes to ride the elevator—about thirty seconds. A marketing message is not to be confused with a mission statement, which gives overarching principles for the business's existence to internal staff as well as to customers. Mission statements are important and are heavily used on websites; they are discussed in depth later on in the book.

In a traditional marketing situation, you would respond to the question "What do you do?" by saying exactly what you do, who you help, and how your audience benefits from what you have to offer. That idea is carried throughout your brochures and other forms of print media.

Website visitors want their messages fast, brief, and crystal clear. Jakob Nielsen's 1997 landmark study of web readability found that 79 percent of web readers always *scan* any new page they come across; only 16 percent read a new page word for word.[3] This information is still relevant today. Consequently, visitors typically enter a site and immediately scan the home page for something that will tell them the site is relevant to their needs or interests.

Developing a Succinct Message

Once you have a clearly defined target audience, it's easy to create a marketing message because you're already tapped into what your audience wants and needs. For impact, your message should contain verbs that indicate assistance and usage. Your job here is to connect the pieces. Avoid passive language in your message. For example, instead of saying, "My service is used by home owners before a storm to prevent their important records from becoming damaged," say, "My business helps home owners save their important documents from storm damage."

Here's an easy "what (verb), whom (ideal client), and how (key benefit)" formula for creating a unique marketing message that will quickly communicate with your target audience:

What do I do? Create [verb] mouthwatering confectionery.

Whom do I serve? People who are celebrating [ideal client].

How specifically do my customers benefit? Transform parties from the simple to the sublime [key result].

The next step is to combine your what, whom, and how: "Renaissance Bakery creates mouthwatering confectioneries that transform your celebrations from the simple to the sublime."

Industry-Specific Tips: Effective Marketing Messages

Professional (marketing company): We help business owners build and sustain relationships with their customers using new media tools.

Healthcare (fitness trainer): I empower women to create individualized nutrition and fitness plans that help them create the bodies they want.

Insurance (health insurance broker): I find affordable health plans for small businesses so they can protect their loved ones at minimum cost.

Support (virtual assistant): I offer office assistance to independent professionals to prevent them from being overwhelmed.

Verbs That Articulate What You Do

Empower	Help	Find
Guarantee	Provide	Match
Connect	Partner	Get
Collaborate	Make	Work
Build	Create	

The advantage of a clear marketing message is that it immediately reaches your audience and defines the benefits you offer. Your blog should display your message on the static portion of the page, e-zines should feature it somewhere on the masthead, and you should begin or end your podcasts with it. Your message should evoke a response such as, "She's talking directly to me—not to *all* entrepreneurs but to me, a nutrition consultant; and she knows exactly what I'm going through. I *must* work with her!"

Remember that your marketing message is dynamic, not static. Consider who you are talking to, and make sure your message is audience appropriate. Also, whenever there's a change in your business product or service, it's time to revise your message.

Part Two

Getting Your Message Across … With a Website

THREE

WEBSITE ESSENTIALS

Today, without an online presence your business is likely to be perceived as nonexistent. Your website is the hub—the gateway to all of your online marketing efforts. It is an integral part of your business identity and your calling card for doing business in the twenty-first century.

All other new media tools—e-zine, blog, and podcast—are most effective when they are associated with and appear on your website. You can directly connect with your customers or prospects and show them everything you have to offer in one convenient place. A website also is an essential lead-generating tool, capturing visitors' contact information and automatically building your authentic customer list—spam free.

One of the most important things that a website does is set the stage for building your brand. When prospects and customers know your brand—what it looks like, what it stands for, and how customers can benefit—it opens the floodgates for easy communication. Nike's Swoosh, in combination with their slogan "Just Do It!" is a good example of how a brand can succinctly convey a business identity. McDonald's Golden Arches and Starbuck's signature green logo with a mermaid all convey brand identity.

Having the same look and feel in your brand across the board is critical.

Creating a seamless integration online and offline will reinforce your brand and set you apart, making you more easily recognizable in the marketplace.

Branding will also help you clearly communicate and cut through information clutter. When you have only limited time to vie for the attention of your customers, branding helps you convey what your business is about quickly, efficiently, and in a meaningful manner.

Your website helps with what you say and how you say it. You can write articles, offer assessments, and communicate with a variety of tools. As the bedrock for your online community, your website is the place where you can poll your audience, interact with your readers in a forum, and find out what makes your customers tick and what keeps them up at night.

Technology Essentials

Say What Your Business Does with a Domain

Your first stop in creating your online presence is choosing a domain name. For solid branding, select a domain name that is the same as your business name. When visitors type in your business name in a search engine, this will give them a good chance of being taken to your corresponding site. Buy a .com extension whenever you can because this has become the standard for business. But remember: Because your domain is part of your brand, protect it by purchasing other extensions if they're available, such as .net, .info, .biz, and .org.

Having multiple domains—purchasing domain names that include your company name, what you do, and your own name—is especially helpful because you want it to be easy for your prospects and customers to remember you and to find you. You can point all of those names to one central website. For example, writer Regan White publishes her pop culture rants and raves on www.reganwhite.com, but also uses www.regansrants.com, the name of her column, to point to her main website.

Many business owners choose their business name before considering whether it would work as a domain name and then run into problems when they can't find the corresponding domain. Some existing business owners who did not purchase their own domain name from the onset of the Internet revolution also tend to run into problems when their name is already taken.

As more individuals and businesses get on the web, .com extensions are becoming scarcer. The result is that more people are using .net, .biz, and others. It's important to remember that in most cases your competitor owns the .com extension and you don't want to send your prospects to them. One way to get around this problem is to incorporate your domain name and its extension into part of your branding. For example, the domain authorworld.com is already taken. If you really want to name your company Author World or have already done so, then use the entire domain name, with a different extension (for example, Author-World.net), as the name of the company and use it in every piece of marketing material you create. If you advertise only "AuthorWorld," then people are likely to automatically assume it's a .com, even though .net is written on the business card.

Consider also registering your domain with a .mobi extension for those who use a mobile handheld device such as a web-enhanced cell phone, Black-Berry, or iPhone. With mobile devices outselling regular personal computers (PCs), it's only a matter of time before .mobi sites become the norm. Even if you don't use it right now, you'll at least have the option to use it in the future.

In the constant scramble for fast-diminishing dot-com names, some business owners use various combinations in their domains that can lead to potential errors. For example, some businesses use a hyphen to secure that dot-com domain extension, but the sale can easily go to the competitor if the prospect searches for the business name without the hyphen. Many business owners use the plural of the domain instead of the singular. Some use the adjective *my* or the article *the* in front of the desired domain or additions such as *online* or *home* after the name. Again, if you do that—then your business name should be MyBusinessName .com, TheBusinessName.com, or BusinessNameOnline.com so that prospects never have to question whether it's indeed your site that they're visiting.

Using your full business name rather than an abbreviated version or initials is best. In case of very long names such as a partnership of lawyers: Barrett, Levine, Coombs, Abercrombie, and Zuckerman, using the first two names are good enough. Avoid using the initials or any other abbreviation that may seem arbitrary.

Consider misspellings or typos of your business name and purchase them as well so you can point them to the correct domain (for example, mega-retailer Amazon.com also bought Amazom.com).

To get a domain name or to find out if the one you want is available, go to any web hosting company's site. Popular options include GoDaddy (www.godaddy .com) and Register.com (www.register.com). If you need help generating ideas for the right domain name or would like to check the availability of several different options at once, try a domain name generator such as nameboy.com.

A word of caution: When you register your domain name, use a Hotmail or Yahoo! account and not your business e-mail address to deter spammers from stealing your information.

Finding a Good Web Host

A web hosting company hosts your site on the Internet so that it's visible to millions of potential customers. A full-featured web host offers an arsenal of marketing tools to help get the word out about your business, from do-it-yourself website builders or templates to e-zine, blog, and podcast integration. Your web hosting company is a one-stop resource, providing the tools that are increasingly necessary to streamline your online activities. Some features are included in the price for web hosting, for example, e-mail addresses tailored to your domain, FTP access, site traffic analytics, and forums. Other features, however, are fee-based add-ons, such as e-commerce tools.

Some web hosts go a step further in becoming an indispensable resource. If you don't have a marketing budget, a web host can provide advice and advanced tools such as search engine optimization to improve your website rankings on Google, Yahoo!, and other search engines.

Don't simply shop around for the lowest price when searching for a web host, because you will get exactly what you pay for. Reliability and dependability should be of utmost concern. Owing to the 24/7 nature of the Internet, you don't know whether someone will visit your site at 3 p.m. or 3 a.m. Consequently, you want to avoid a host that frequently shuts down its sites for unscheduled maintenance or to fix glitches.

Security is also of paramount concern. A good host will offer ways to make your site secure, using encryption or a SSL certificate, and will help visitors coming to your site be more willing to share their information. If you sell a product or service from your site, a host that offers a secure shopping cart feature is crucial.

If you are going to use all of the new media components—e-zines, blogs, and podcasts—then you will definitely need a host that offers plenty of storage space. You may want to start small but be able to add on as your archive grows.

A web hosting company that also offers multiple e-mail addresses will be beneficial so you can compartmentalize your information. For example, you may want dedicated e-mail addresses such as sales@yourdomain.com and seminars@yourdomain.com. You may also have an e-mail address to catch everything else.

If you feel even the slightest bit confused about the vast array of features, call your host's customer service number and tell the agent what you want to do with your site. He or she should be able to help you choose the right features for your business.

Regardless of the type of business you own, a full-service website host will offer your site a solid foundation to house all your new media components.

Web Hosting Providers

GO DADDY
As one of the nation's largest web hosting companies, GoDaddy (www.godaddy .com) offers everything a business could want and more. It's reliable; they offer

superior customer service and support all the new media components. They also offer full e-commerce capabilities.

YAHOO!

As one of the oldest web hosts around, Yahoo! (www.yahoo.com) offers hundreds of website templates and site builders. Yahoo! has branded itself as a small business solutions company. Their monthly fee is higher than that of other companies, but they offer many features. Yahoo! may be a good choice for a new entrepreneur because its templates are low-tech.

BLUEHOST

BlueHost (www.bluehost.com) offers a full variety of features, but what makes it stand out is the ease of integration with other new media products, including WordPress blogs. With lifetime domains and great customer service, they are a solid bet.

Template or Custom Website?

Once you've registered your domain, you'll have to decide whether you should use a template or custom-designed website; there are benefits and drawbacks with each choice. A custom website is a unique site that is tailored specifically for your business and created by a web designer. Having a designer create your site for you can free up your time so that you can focus on what you do best: working on your business. However, a custom site is generally expensive, and you'll likely pay monthly maintenance costs. Furthermore, you may have to wait until your site is up and running.

Today's website templates are so sophisticated and aesthetically pleasing that often you cannot distinguish them from a customized site. Templates are also easy and affordable; they allow you to create a professional website even if you have little design experience. You can customize a template by using a unique header created by a graphic designer. You can easily maintain a website built by a template, and you can make changes to it anytime. One drawback is limited design flexibility; furthermore, you won't have a personal technician who knows the ins and outs of your site.

Both a custom site and a template can provide an effective business website solution.

Core Essentials

Now that you have taken care of the technical aspects of connecting with your audience, it's time to get to the core of your business to determine what to say and how to say it with your website. When you create an organic small business, you have the opportunity to develop a business that communicates on an authentic level. Using this principle, your website can emphasize integrity and professionalism. It's imperative to convey values on your website. These must be organic values that come from your core; ones that relate to you and your business.

How to Convey Important Values

Let visitors know who you are and why they should do business with you. These values should be dispersed throughout the content of your site. All businesses should strive to convey basic values such as reliability, integrity, professionalism, and commitment to their clients. Which values you'll want to emphasize most heavily depends on your specific business industry.

Industry-Specific Tips: Values

Healthcare and social assistance: Caring, empathy, attention to detail

Manufacturing: Durability, timeliness, quality

Waste management: Efficiency, environmental sensitivity

Food service: Freshness, cleanliness, economical

Accommodation: Safety, comfort, cleanliness

Construction: Durability, quality, safety

Retail trade: Cost competitive, aesthetically conscious, customer aware

Arts: Inspire, provoke, motivate, delight

Creating a Mission Statement for Your Business

As a small business owner, you want to honor your own authenticity and integrate your values into your mission statement. A mission statement shows potential customers the purpose for your business and the values your business respects and abides by. This umbrella statement is the underlying force that drives or fuels your business.

People do business with those they feel comfortable with. Your mission statement will attract customers that align with your mission—these are the customers that will become part of your community. You will likely not serve those people who are not aligned with your statement. It's important to remember that you cannot and should not try to serve the entire universe. In keeping with the tenets of organic small business marketing, it is okay if there are some people who will pass you by because they are not aligned with your truth. Focusing on serving the people who resonate with what you offer will result in greater happiness and fulfillment.

Internally, the mission statement shows you where you want your business to go. Focus on the main goal that drives your business. For example, a carting company has many goals—to make money, to be efficient, and to provide their workers with good wages—but their main underlying goal could be to be sensitive to the environment. Because this is the company's driving purpose, it needs to be reflected in its mission statement.

A mission statement should contain three important components: your business, your purpose or goal, and your values. A good mission statement is motivational and is only about three or four sentences long. If it can fit on the back of your business card, then it's the right length.

To guide you in developing your mission statement, brainstorm with yourself or other business stakeholders. You must know and be able to communicate the following: What do you do? Why are you in business? What do you stand for?

What benefits do your customers receive? Those benefits are a direct outgrowth of your values. For example, if you own a bed and breakfast and you value comfort, your guests will benefit from a clean and safe environment.

Consider the values that you feel are important to you and your business and your ultimate goal and then integrate them into your mission statement. After you define the three components of a mission statement, write and rewrite a mission statement that seamlessly reflects the guiding principles that direct your business.

Sample Mission Statement

New Media Mavens' Mission (www.newmediamavens.com): Our mission is to help small business owners use new media to promote who they are, so they can increase visibility, credibility, and profitability in an authentic way.

Action Words to Use in Your Mission Statement

Improve	Organize	Create
Empower	Solve	Change
Collaborate	Invent	Furnish
Reinvent	Educate	Assist
Maintain	Promote	Support
Incorporate	Develop	Encourage
Fulfill	Instill	Supply

Create Compelling Content

In today's world, most customers will never walk into your physical store or office, but they will get an impression of you and your business by checking you out virtually. Your website—the workhorse of your business—must be aesthetically pleasing, technologically sound, and speak to your audience directly and quickly.

How to Say It: Verbal

Your website's content must speak to your audience's needs. Whether your audience is made up of doctors, lawyers, accountants, homeowners, home-based workers, children, or teenagers, your objective is to address their needs, their pain, their challenges, and what's keeping them up at night. For example, an accountant knows that many entrepreneurs have a hard time keeping the financial aspects of their business in order. The accountant's home page could address her target audience's need directly: "Spend more time on what you do best and leave the rest (your books) to me." This marketing message is displayed prominently and is one of the first things you'd see on her website.

While you're offering solutions and advice, opt for a conversational writing style addressing your prospect directly with the word *you* instead of using less personal words such as *customers*, *businesspeople*, and *prospects*. Also be aware that content must be written with your customer in mind. Keep the focus on the benefits the customer will receive.

Conversational doesn't mean careless copy that is riddled with common modifiers such as *really* and *very*. Your goal should be to keep the site's language short and concise. Instead of strengthening the message, modifiers tend to dilute and weaken what you're saying. Really! Remember, the language on your site should be casual but still business professional.

Another thing to be aware of is the use of clichés such as *quick as lightning*, *red as a rose*, *cold as ice*, and *hot as fire*. It's one thing to try to cleverly turn a phrase, but clichés are amateurish and don't enhance your text. Finding the right tone that is unique to your business and personality is the key.

When it comes to copy on the web, conciseness rules. Because 79 percent of web visitors only scan web pages, it makes sense to use relevant headlines and sub-headlines to guide the reader along as he or she checks out your pages. Headlines must pull readers in and compel your prospects to learn more. They should describe the content that follows.

Headlines are most effective when they trigger readers' needs and emotions. Look over the following universal emotional triggers and sample headings.

Emotional Trigger: Convenience

Gift basket company: We'll customize your gift and even deliver it for you.

Cleaning service: You have better things to do than clean your house.

Pet sitter: We'll take care of your pets while you work.

Emotional Trigger: Immortality

Community church: Leading the way into the Kingdom of Heaven.

Cosmetic surgeon: Turn back the hands of time with a [procedure].

Emotional Trigger: Fear

Computer technician: Never lose valuable data again.

Funeral home: Don't burden loved ones when the inevitable happens.

Emotional Trigger: Love

Florist: Flowers and love go hand in hand.

Jewelry store: With diamonds, your love will shine forever.

Emotional Trigger: Envy

Car dealer: Trade up to a [luxury car brand].

Home decorator: Live like you are rich! With your own furnishings.

Hairdresser: Want to look like a top model? Get long, luxuriant hair now.

Emotional Trigger: Beauty

Nail salon: Put your best foot forward with a spa pedicure.

Spa owner: Feel beautiful inside and out—revitalizing mind and body.

Emotional Trigger: Scarcity

Bed and breakfast: Enjoy full patio breakfasts: summer months only.

Emotional Trigger: Health

Chiropractor: Get back relief today...not tomorrow.

Emotional Trigger: Curiosity

Health food store: Stop the aging process in its tracks.

Holistic healer: Miracle cures: The best kept secrets.

Book marketing consultant: Secrets to getting published.

Wholesaler: Exporter reveals hidden markets.

Baseball card collector: Trading tips for the best cards.

In an effort to be concise, many business owners drastically reduce what they write on their website, leaving out salient aspects that will appeal to their audience. Write just enough copy to convey your message. The objective is to get to the core of what you do in the least amount of words as possible. At the same time, ensure that your text is meaningful. Don't write about apples when you should be talking about oranges. Get to the point.

In this time-crunched world, customers don't want to read a laundry list of features. Focus on benefits, results, and solutions that you offer. *Features* describe your product or service but don't convey what benefits they offer to the customer. For example, "Elizabeth Buckley sells a health tonic loaded with vitamins." This feature-laden statement can be changed to emphasize the benefits: "Elizabeth Buckley sells a disease-curing elixir."

Once you write copy that you are confident taps into your visitors' needs, the next step is to establish your credibility. Most people are wary of buying from or working with people they don't know; therefore, it's important to establish trust. Provide proof that you are the expert and the best person for the job with testimonials, awards, and a portfolio of your work, if applicable. You can also list any relevant associations or organizations to which you belong and provide a biography with your relevant experience and education. It helps the credibility factor and makes your content most compelling when you offer an incentive for people to use your service or purchase your product. Some incentives are a free trial, a limited time offer, and a complimentary consultation.

How to Say It: Nonverbal

In addition to communicating with your words, the colors, fonts, and images you use on your website set the tone for your business. When communicating with your audience, remember that nonverbal communication is important on the web.

When using a template, use colors that harmonize with your existing marketing materials to keep a consistent look. Pick a customizable template so you can upload your own unique header. Many times it can be difficult to find an exact color match; however, you can get quite close to the color scheme used in your print materials. Better yet, hire a web designer who can create an exact color match to your offline promotions and develop a personalized site.

Perceptions for Businesses

Because 90 percent of communication is nonverbal, color plays an important role. Like scent, color evokes an emotional response. Although there are some can't-miss choices, don't be afraid to be authentic and experiment with colors that resonate for you. The following list provides the traditional meanings of common colors and suggests compatible business usage:

Pink: Romance, love, friendship, delicacy, feminine; ideal for relationship coaches, florists, and breast cancer awareness sites

Purple: Royalty, spiritual, transformation, creativity, new age; ideal for spirituality-based or new age businesses and businesses in the creative realm

Blue: Solid, communication, calm, wisdom, trust, reassuring; ideal for financial businesses, insurance companies, and lawyers

Green: Growth, money, abundance, fertility, freshness, health, environment; ideal for grocers, environmental businesses, therapists, healthcare businesses

Red: Energy, strength, passion; ideal for bold businesses based on power and for professionals; use in combination with black

Black: Power, sophisticated, elegant, formal, style, dramatic, serious; ideal for fine dining establishments; commonly used as an accent color

Gold and yellow: Wealth, wisdom, prestige, power, energy, joy, clarity, light, intelligence, optimism; ideal for the construction industry

White: Purity, goodness, simplicity, clean; ideal for almost every business

Brown: Friendship, earthy, comfort, content, reliable, sturdy; ideal for businesses involved in administrative support

Orange: Vibrant, enthusiasm, energy, warmth; ideal for creative businesses and teachers

Gray: Security, staid, quality, professional, stable; ideal for the legal industry

LOGO AND HEADER

The colors in your logo set the stage for your entire website's color scheme. One way to extend your brand is to create a header with your logo. A header is like a banner that sits atop your web pages. It's also a handy way to visually connect your other new media products—blog, podcast, e-zine—to your website by linking directly to them on your header.

You can have a graphic designer create a unique banner to incorporate your logo, text, and other elements. A header is an aesthetic creation that should be pleasing and convey your brand as soon as someone visits your site. It's a great way to make a website built by a template look unique.

IMAGES

Use images as well as boldface text to organize and enhance your copy and convey the appropriate tone of your message. As the old saying goes, a picture is worth a thousand words. Make sure your images correspond to the text and are appropriate to the business you offer. For example, an audiologist shouldn't use a picture of a woman holding her glasses because the spotlight should be on hearing.

You can use your own pictures or find appropriate ones on the numerous free stock image sites on the Internet. Browse the images at sites like www.sxc.hu or use the images provided by your site builder. Image files should be in jpg, png, or gif format. For the fastest download, keep them less than 100 kb (kilobytes). Most photos on the web range from 30 to 65 kb. When considering resolution, 72 dpi (dots per inch) is standard. Photos need to load quickly and be clear.

SPECIAL EFFECTS

If you choose to use a special effect for the introductory page for your website, be sure to offer a way to skip the video (or other effect). Web users who don't have a high-speed connection might not want to wait to download your graphics. If you use special effects within your website pages, use them judiciously.

Make sure they relate specifically to what you are talking about and make sure they download quickly. Nothing will have your customer click away faster than slow-loading graphics.

The advent of digital cameras has made photos much more accessible to the public. In the early days of the Internet, clip art or cartoons dominated the web. These graphics are now best relegated to businesses that want to portray a whimsical approach.

Strive for balance on your website. A professional can help you create a design aesthetic. If you don't know anything about design, find a web designer who will help you balance the ratio of text to images.

FONTS

Some designers like to use tiny text on websites—text that is too small for the majority of the population to read. If people have to squint to read your site, they will click away fast! The standard for most websites is 10 pitch; 12-pitch type or larger conveys an elementary feeling and may be too large for online copy.

For text, use web fonts such as Verdana and Arial, which work on all browsers on PCs and Macs. When designing your website's header, you can get more creative and use uncommon and/or or fancy fonts to create the effect or mood you want.

How to Say It on the Five Standard Pages of a Website

Compelling content should be dispersed throughout your entire site. Most business websites have at least five main or standard pages, and each should be accessible via a standard navigation bar: home, services or products, about, testimonials, and contact. Common extra pages include articles, FAQs, resources, links, and events and news. You may want to add other pages that appeal to your audience.

Create a Logical Navigation System

Logical navigation makes your site user-friendly. Imagine you are a gracious host welcoming guests to your home. You want them to feel comfortable right away. You direct them to where they should sit, show them the restroom and even the kitchen. Your website is your online home, so treat your guests with care. Show them where your information is and use consistent navigation that remains the same on every page of your website.

Simple and easy navigation is your first priority if you want a website that will be useful to your visitors. Navigation should be instinctive and intuitive. Users shouldn't have to work or think to get the information they want from your site; if they do, they will likely try a different site. Users always want to know where they are on your site. Make sure your logo or company name is visible on every page. They want to know the areas they have already visited on your site. Your browser's "back menu" should track this. Users also want to know where else they can go. You can provide links either on your navigation bar or embedded in your text directing your readers where to go.

Here's a true story of a navigation nightmare to illustrate the importance of answering those three questions: A visitor entered a site and couldn't find the information she needed. She had to think, "What do I do next?" She randomly clicked on a link, but it took her somewhere she didn't want to go. She wanted to go back but couldn't find a link to the home page. Panicked, she looked at her web browser, and the arrow to go back was deactivated. No help there. She was stuck. She had just entered the web Twilight Zone!

This scenario doesn't have to happen. Every page on your website should have a visible navigation bar—positioned at the top or left side of the screen (and it should be at the same place on each page). Avoid filling the navigation

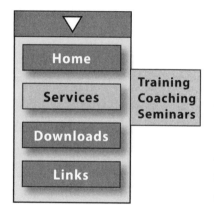

bar with more than six to seven links. Instead, use a secondary navigation bar that pulls out of the main bar or use a secondary stand-alone bar at the bottom of the page. Also, the main navigation links should be named after the broadest categories; use subcategories, if necessary. It's important that users know exactly where they are and where they've been on your site. Links that change color after a visitor has clicked on them indicate where the reader has been and are an expected feature of today's website.

The broad categories shown in the illustration above are home, services, downloads, and links. When visitors hover their pointer over the services button, for example, they see the training, coaching, and seminars links pull out from the main navigation bar.

Knowing what your audience wants and what they're looking for and providing it to them quickly and efficiently are key principles to keep in mind when designing your navigation system. It's always a good idea to provide a site map so users can see, at a glance, all the pages within your site. Most do-it-yourself site builders will incorporate this feature, or ask your web designer.

The Home Page

Your home page is key to the success of your website. It is the hardest working page because it identifies your target audience, attracts and sustains your visitors' attention, and leads readers to the next step in the buying process. The home page is usually the first page that your visitor sees when he or she browses directly to your site, but this is not necessarily so. It depends on what the visitor searched for. A search engine could take a visitor directly to your contact page, articles, or the about us page. You never know what page your

Navigation Checklist

Here's a checklist to ensure navigation ease on your website:

Navigation bar text: My navigation bar is large enough
and the text font is clear enough to be easily read.　　　　____ Yes ____ No

Navigation bar position: My navigation bar is positioned
in the usual place (top or left).　　　　____ Yes ____ No

Links: All my links work and connect to the correct page.　　　　____ Yes ____ No

Secondary navigation bar: I have a secondary navigation
bar (usually at the bottom of the page).　　　　____ Yes ____ No

visitors will land on so make sure each page is filled with specific and compelling content. Even though visitors may enter through the back door—from other pages on your site—they'll inevitably go to your home page to get the big picture, to see what you and your business are all about.

Many web visitors don't click beyond a site's home page. They often don't have time or patience to figure out what your site is about. They have too many options, so you have to capture their interest immediately. The first lines on your home page should clearly identify who your product or service is targeted to and the benefits. This is where your marketing message speaks to them and where you convince them that you can help.

The marketing message can be woven into the copy at the top of your home page. It can be in your header and/or in the first lines of text that a visitor reads. Wherever you put it, your message needs to be prominent so that potential customers know immediately who you serve, what you do, and what the benefits of your products and services are. You can also accomplish this with headlines. For example, you can name your ideal customers. Consider using a headline that says "Attention coaches, consultants, and speakers." Your copy should then focus on the challenges that they face and how you can offer solutions. Provide an easily identifiable link to your products or services page so visitors can learn more about what you provide. All this information should be in the top third portion of your home page.

OPT-IN BOX

The home page is an ideal page to prominently display an opt-in box for your visitors to join your e-mail list and receive reports, e-books, articles, or tips that shed light on their challenges. An opt-in box is a simple box that is common on many sites. It asks for a user name and e-mail address so your visitors can receive information from you. For your part, this feature automatically creates a database so you can easily send out materials and build your community. This sharing of information continues to offer your visitors value and helps cement your relationship long after they leave your site.

Remember that privacy is of paramount importance. It is imperative that you ask your readers' permission before sending them any kind of information about your product or even free tips. There are two levels of privacy security that keep your database protected.

The first is known as a single opt-in, which occurs when a customer visits your website and types in his or her e-mail address to start receiving information about your product. For a double opt-in, first a customer types in his or her e-mail address. Then your web host sends out a standard e-mail to confirm the customer's wish to receive mail from you. After your website gets the confirmation, you will be able to send out promotional materials. The double opt-in authentication is rapidly becoming an industry standard because it provides increased security against spam.

OPT-IN INCENTIVE

If possible, provide an information product to your customers. Introduce this service with an irresistible headline and display a link or an opt-in box prominently on your home page. Such a product is a powerful incentive for prospective customers to give you their name and e-mail address. And once you get their contact information, they become a part of your authentic customer list and valued members of your community.

Industry-Specific Tips: Information Products and Headlines

Construction (handyman): Provide a tip a week via e-mail—Get Handy Household Tips in Your E-mail When You Need Them!

Professional services (intellectual property attorney): Offer a free white paper—Copyright Information You Must Know Before You Sell Your Books, Music, or Art.

Retail trade (clothing boutique): Promote special sales and give tips to executives and professionals—Sign up to Receive News on Upcoming Promotions and Discounts; Download Free Bonus Booklet, "How to Dress Business Casual."

Healthcare (nutritionist): Write an informational article—Is Your Body Getting the Right Nutrients? Find Out Now!

Real estate (real estate agent): Provide a location-specific guide—Download Your Complete Community Guide to Shops, Schools, Restaurants, Churches and More!

Financial (bookkeeper): Target single professional women—Get Your *Free* Audio, "How Single Women Can Save a Bundle on Their Taxes" Download Immediately.

Administrative and support (web designer): Offer an e-book—Instant Download: "101 Ways to Attract Visitors to Your Website and Keep Them Coming Back!"

Once your web visitor types in her user name and e-mail address, the opt-in box works behind the scenes to add the information to your database. Next, it delivers a preformatted letter (customized by you) thanking her for signing up and providing a link to confirm that she wants to be on your list. After your customer has completed the double opt-in procedure then make sure to deliver the promised information product. Use standard formats—send audio as an mp3 file and provide articles, tip sheets, and e-books in PDF format or as a Word file. An option is to send your customer a link to a subscribers page that contains your promotional material.

Get visitors to provide their e-mail addresses by conducting contests or sweepstakes or to have drawings for prizes. Or consider making some pages available only to visitors who register or log in to your site.

BONUS INCENTIVE: ASSESSMENTS

Another way to capture visitors' contact information is to provide a self-scoring assessment on your home page. The assessment should provide your clients with insights after they complete it. To view the answers and evaluation, visitors must enter their e-mail address. Assessments can help your website visitors decide whether your product or service is right for them. For example, a book marketing consultant could have an assessment titled "Are You Ready to Get Published?" The assessment asks the visitor ten questions that determine his or her level of readiness. To get the results, the visitor must type in a user name and valid e-mail address. This type of assessment offers you a double benefit: You not only have added a valid client but have learned something about that client, which can help you provide individualized service. Moreover, your customer also discovers valuable information about the next step in the publishing process.

An assessment can be used for businesses that offer both products and services. It is an organic tool that you offer your prospects whether or not they become your immediate customers. One of the most popular assessment generators is found at www.assessmentgenerator.com; for a monthly fee you can purchase a customizable assessment for almost every kind of business.

Your goal for your home page is to establish your credibility as the go-to person for your visitors' needs. Consequently, it is the perfect place to display membership and association icons and to post your best testimonial (along with a link to a complete testimonials page).

Avoid crowding your home page with purchase buttons and other product material. Establish a relationship first. Interacting with your customer on your site should be organic—not forced—a naturally evolving process. This means your website's navigation bar and hyperlinks embedded in the body text must reflect a logical flow leading deeper into the other pages of your site.

Size matters. The copy on your home page needs to be short. Visitors should not have to scroll down to see the majority of content on any page, especially your home page. Keep all the important elements—such as your image header, navigation bar, marketing message and your opt-in box—above the point at which your customer has to scroll down.

The Products or Services Page

While your home page should concisely describe what your site offers, your products or services page should go in-depth. This is where you get specific, but avoid offering everything plus the kitchen sink because too much information can be overwhelming. Time is of the essence. Customers should not have to search through your products or services page to find your offerings. The onus is on you to provide important information in as appealing a manner as possible.

One way to organize information on this page is to categorize your offerings into main headings and subheadings using different fonts, type sizes, or formatting (such as boldface or colored text). Most sites use large fonts for headings. A 2007 Poynter Institute/Eyetrack III study[4] revealed that "when a headline is larger than its accompanying blurb text, it's perceived as the important element of the headline-blurb block—so people appear to decide that viewing the headline is sufficient and they skip the blurb." You want people to read the text in your blurb, so make your headlines pop by distinguishing them from the text, but don't make them vastly different.

It's important to keep the headings consistent. All main headings should look identical. Subheadings should also look identical to each other but different from the main headings. For example, a training consultant could use "Seminars" as a main heading, setting it off by using boldface or colored text. Underneath that heading he would describe the seminars he conducts in a short blurb. Subheadings in a different (usually smaller) font would divide the remaining text. Examples of secondary headings for this site are "Productivity" and "Personal Development." Another main heading this consultant could use is "Coaching," which would look like the previous main heading. Under this heading he would give an overview of his coaching practice and then provide further information under the subheadings "Executive Coaching" and "Individual Life Coaching."

Another idea is to feature either your most expensive or least expensive product or service first, depending on what you think will attract your target audience. Some business owners use a funnel-like approach, by which they start with the least expensive product and then present the next higher-priced item, building to the most expensive. For example, if a customer likes the $25 product, she's more likely to return to purchase your $100 item and eventually the $400 item. Ultimately, it comes down to knowing your customers and determining what will appeal to them. If you are targeting wholesalers, you may want to emphasize delivery speed and the capability to purchase in bulk as factors affecting your customers' purchase decisions.

After you've organized and described your products or services, you need to make the buying process as easy as possible for your customers. It's important to offer a way to make immediate purchases. One easy way is to set up a PayPal account so customers can use a familiar secure method of payment. Whether you use a service like PayPal or set up your site to receive credit card payments, be sure to give clear instructions and lead your customers through the buying process.

About Us Page

A website gives a lot of important information about your company. It tells who you serve and what you offer, how to purchase, and how to build a relationship with you. But visitors don't want to do business with an anonymous website; they want to know the person behind the site.

An about us page is now a standard part of all business websites. It should be labeled simply on the navigation bar; most sites use the title "About Us," but you could modify this to "About [Name of Company]," "About Me," or even just "About." Do not use a creative title for your link—such as "Info Page," "Biography," "Company"—because it will be unfamiliar to your visitors.

Because visitors can't look you in the eye or gauge your handshake to determine your trustworthiness, credibility is a major issue that you must overcome before you can do business on the Internet. The about us page serves to reassure potential customers that you have genuine credentials and to inform them that you are qualified to offer your product or service. Credentials include academic degrees, professional degrees and accreditations, awards and special recognitions, and professional affiliations. Be sure to include any relevant experiences or information that boosts your trustworthiness. For example, describe how you got started in the business and provide any relevant facts and statistics, the number of years you've been in business, the size of your company, and the number of projects you've completed.

Industry-Specific Tips: About Us
Construction: "My construction career started with learning from the best: my father. During my summer breaks, I used to work on the job learning how to lay foundation and put up drywall so that it doesn't

crack. That kind of experience created a legacy of learning that I continue with my own son. We create luxurious homes that we live in ourselves."

Healthcare (plastic surgeon): "I graduated from XYZ University magna cum laude with a degree in chemistry. I studied medicine at [Name of University] and interned at [Name of Hospital], where I also did my residency. I spent several summers volunteering for Doctors Without Borders, correcting harelip deformities in a number of communities in India and Africa."

Wholesale trade: "We offer the finest quality gems at great value. Resting on three generations of wholesale experience, every member of our team is trained to our exacting standards. We are members of the International Diamond Federation and all of our diamonds are 'conflict-free.'"

After you've posted relevant content that gives your visitor a close-up view of who is behind the site, the icing on the cake is to add your photograph. A professional head shot is best, but don't rule out an on-site photo that shows you involved in your work. Some business owners go all the way and add audio or a video to their about us page to engage visitors even more.

Testimonial Page

Testimonials are comments from your customers who have been satisfied with your product or service. Such statements enhance your credibility and can be the ultimate persuaders. To make them even more powerful, add a photograph of the person giving the testimonial so the website visitor knows the reviewer is real. If the customer is local, pack your digital camera and pay your customer a visit. Take a photo in his or her environment.

When creating your testimonial page, place the most enthusiastic quotes first. Try to offer some diversity: Praise should come from men and women, from several geographic locations, and relate to a variety of your products and services. Update your testimonials often by adding new ones; a good rule of thumb is that each time you get a new testimonial, update the page and remove an older one.

For maximum effect, some business owners add audio, along with the written text of the customer raving about his or her outstanding experience with the company. This is easy to do using readily available providers such as audiostrategies.com or audioacrobat.com. Make sure your recording does not play automatically when the page is loaded, because this can be highly annoying. Instead, offer a click-to-hear-audio link or button.

Some people never get to the testimonial page, so it's a good idea to disperse your testimonials throughout your website. Even though you have a dedicated testimonial page, make sure you have at least one relevant statement per page and a link that leads visitors to read your other testimonials. For example, if you offer a product and you have a testimonial that refers directly to that product, put the comment on the same page and in close proximity to the product you're selling. Place the comment in a shaded or breakout box to make it stand out from the other content on the page.

If a prospect is on the fence about a purchasing decision, a good resounding testimonial can be the deal maker.

How Not to Say It with Testimonials

Don't pile *all* of your testimonials on one page. Place them at relevant points on different pages.

Don't post the entire testimonial if it's long. Create a read-more link that takes the visitor to the full quote on your testimonial page.

Don't change a customer's testimonial, unless it's to correct an obvious grammar or spelling mistake.

Some people feel shy about asking their customers for a testimonial, but it can be as simple as sending a straightforward e-mail. For example, a small business owner of a tutoring service could send an e-mail to the satisfied parents asking them these questions: (1) What was your child's situation before working with us? (2) How did we solve your situation? (3) What was the outcome? (4) Any other comments?

Request a testimonial at the high point of service, especially when your customer significantly benefits from your efforts. At this point, he or she will be in the best frame of mind to give you raving comments. Most people, though, ask for a testimonial at the conclusion of the service, and that's fine, too. Present your request as a win-win situation for your customer by offering to include a link to his or her website on your page.

You can also send a simple template to your customers such as the one shown in the box below.

Step-by-Step Testimonial Request Template

Dear [Customer's Name]:

It's been a pleasure working with you these past weeks. In order to continue maintaining a high standard of service, I periodically monitor customer feedback. Please take a few minutes to jot down your thoughts and e-mail them back to me. I appreciate your comments.

What are three benefits that you get from working with [your Company's Name]?

How would you recommend us to others? What would you say?

In what ways did we provide the solutions that you needed?

May we use your comments as a testimonial on our website? We'd be happy to include a link to your website and mention your business name to promote your site.

Contact Us Page

It may seem like a no-brainer to include a page with your contact information, but some websites forgo this vital page altogether. The contact page provides an important communication gateway through which visitors can get in touch with you, asking questions or offering feedback. Visitors to your website are more likely to contact you if you make it as easy as possible. Don't make customers search for your phone number and e-mail address. In addition to offering your own contact information, a good contact us page is an opportunity to learn more about your audience. An e-mail form on this page should ask visitors questions such as, *How did you hear about us?* and *How would you prefer to be contacted?*

A contact us page is standard in most site-builder templates. If your site is custom created, your web designer can generate this page. If you are building your own site, then you can get the codes for a contact form through your web hosting company or from a variety of sites on the Internet.

Your web designer or your site-building template will ensure that when visitors type into your contact form the information is immediately sent to you via e-mail. It's a good idea to add a simple autoresponder for comments left in your contact form. The automatically generated message, sent via e-mail, lets visitors who inquire about your services know that you will contact them within twenty-four hours. Even though your customers know they've received a form letter, the quick response demonstrates your professionalism and commitment—important aspects of organic small business marketing.

Remember too that although you have a contact us page, always list an address and phone number on every page of your site. This reassures visitors that you are a real person.

Add-on Pages Directed to Your Target Audience

In addition to the five standard pages that every website should have, think about creating other value-added pages. Such pages could include forums,

FAQs, resources, and events/news to provide a wealth of knowledge for your customers and prospects as well as help you attract more visitors to your site.

FORUMS PAGE

The forums page is where your community meets to ask questions, post comments, discuss industry information, and interact with you and other community members in an informal setting. There are a number of ways to build a community using your website.

Using the forums page provided by your web hosting provider, welcome your community by inviting visitors to discuss their challenges and concerns as they relate to the subject matter of your business. For example, a company that sells baby strollers might invite their community of young parents to discuss both the challenges and the rewards that go with parenthood.

Consider creating discussions about four or five topics that all relate back to your business. Community members can start their own discussion threads among themselves on the forum. A nice touch is to let your community know that you are moderating the forum and will be online at a specific date and time to respond to their concerns or comments.

FAQs

It's usually a good idea to include an FAQ page on your website. *FAQ* stands for "frequently asked questions," and savvy customers will look for this page on your site. Try to anticipate questions potential customers will have and compile others from correspondence you've had with existing clients. Then provide the answers to these questions on your FAQ page. Formulate questions and answers that provide you an opportunity to outline your business process, your style, your costs, and other pertinent information.

RESOURCES

If you create a resources page, your website visitors will have a place to access supplemental information. You can call this page "Resources" or "Freebies," if that suits your target audience. On this page, provide tools, analytics, forecasting calculators, or any related information that your target audience will want.

EVENTS/NEWS

Although you will want to mention important news or events on your home page, provide a link to a separate web page where you can provide the details. An events or news page is a great place to promote a sale or a seminar, to inform visitors that you've been mentioned in the press, and to spotlight anything new in your business.

FOUR

TELLING YOUR AUDIENCE ABOUT YOUR WEBSITE

Many small business owners complain that they've spent a lot of money to produce a beautiful website and it just sits there in cyberspace. No one visits. But without an effort to promote your website you won't increase traffic. Most people agree that the number one way to promote any new media tool (websites, e-zines, blogs, podcasts) is with search engines. While search engines are discussed in-depth in Part Six, this section offers additional concepts and tools to promote your site.

The Power of Free

The word *free* is powerful in any language, and when you combine your free offering with value, your site becomes *sticky*, or memorable; and visitors will return for the solutions you offer. Unfortunately, the words *free* and *free offer* have been so abused on the Internet that they are usually caught by spam filters in most e-mail programs. Thus you should avoid using the word *free* in the subject line of any e-mail message. Within the body of your message, try using other words to convey the same meaning: *sample, trial, complimentary,* and *gift* are alternate choices. The goal is to get customers to want to sample your service without coming across as gimmicky.

Information products for download typically include articles, e-books, videos, tip sheets, checklists, reports, e-mail courses, teleseminars in mp3 format, white papers, booklets, book excerpts, webinars, assessments, e-zines, and podcasts. Giving away information on your site shows your prospects and customers that you care about solving their challenges. It positions you as the expert in your field and the go-to person for solutions. At the same time, the information product serves to educate clients about your business and how you can solve their problems.

By giving away valuable information you can spread the word about your business by embedding your company and contact information into your giveaway. On the last page you can direct readers to your website for further information. Your information stays around for a long time and even gets forwarded so others can share in the value.

A word of caution: Avoid making your information product a blatant advertisement for your products and services. The focus must be on benefits for your target audience.

Industry-Specific Tips: Product Giveaways

Construction (plumber): Do-it-yourself instructions for unclogging a drain, project instructions for changing a showerhead, tip sheet for conserving water; **visitors will be eager to learn from the expert**.

Professional service (career coach): Tip sheet on how to dress for an interview, article on the advantages of joining professional organizations; **potential clients will want to know more**.

Retail trade (gift store): Article on this season's trends in color and style, list of traditional gifts for each wedding anniversary, downloadable coupon; **visitors will turn to you to learn the latest fads**.

Food service (caterer): Tip sheet on how to set up a buffet with a short instructional video, two recipes for a children's party, sample menu for a wedding; **your target audience will perceive you as versatile for any occasion.**

Religious (adult outreach committee): Downloadable audio sermons, weekly e-mail courses on current issues; **busy or indisposed parishioners will be grateful for the chance to stay in touch.**

Healthcare (personal trainer): Tips for avoiding overtraining, article on whether it is okay to exercise when you're sick; **potential clients will see you as a caring individual.**

Real estate (Realtor for single-family dwellings): Article on inexpensive ways to spruce up your property, mortgage rate calculator; **potential home clients will learn to rely on your expertise.**

Financial and insurance (tax accountant): Fact sheet listing new tax laws; reminders to send in quarterly tax payments; **potential clients see that you are organized, responsive and current in your field.**

Administrative and support (employee liaison): Article on how to work with temporary staff, list of simple exercises for avoiding repetitive stress injuries; **clients will look to you for ways to better interact with their employees.**

Promoting Your Website

You can harness the power of free and give away information products as you spread the word about your website across the Internet. You can also employ a variety of other tactics to specifically promote your website, including: writing a simple article and submitting it so your site gets noticed; promoting your site using a linking strategy; and using simple e-mail functions to promote your business to your customers and prospects over and over.

Articles Promotion

Writing articles about your expertise promotes your website like a powerful magnet pulling visitors to your site. If you provide visitors with the information they need and want, articles will serve to boost your credibility and expert status.

You don't have to be the next Shakespeare or Melville or even an aspiring writer to communicate with your target audience. Your articles don't need to sell anything but should share your expertise and your know-how. If you can define five or seven steps to do anything in your business, you can write an article. Once you have a topic, create a simple and informative headline: "How to [procedure]." When describing the steps, write naturally, the way you speak. Other good articles offer tips, reveal industry "secrets," discuss best practices, and present your own hands-on experience. You can even write up case studies (analyses of why certain practices work or don't) or your own assessment of some aspect of your profession.

Every business professional has enough know-how to write an article. For example, if your organization is part of the social assistance industry, you could offer much-needed information to other nonprofits to help maximize resources. You might consider an article that not only lists available homeless shelters but also churches and civic institutions that offer additional beds and shelter during periods of particularly harsh weather. If your business is in the technical services field, you could discuss the practical applications of a study published in a recent professional journal.

The owner of a small advertising company could analyze the underpinnings for a multinational campaign and discuss what elements could be applied to local and regional campaigns. For example, the article could assess how the Martin Agency created the popular Geico advertising campaign, which changed the rules of advertising by creating several simultaneous advertising campaigns for a company (the gecko, the caveman, and the celebrity parody). Every business and industry has plenty of material. To find great content, examine your own business practices and pay attention to trends in your profession.

You can even look to pop culture and create links to publicly available stories and ideas in an original way. This is a great way to create fresh, compelling content for your articles page. A plastic surgeon who specializes in skin grafting could examine the trend of celebrity tattoos and discuss the medical impact of having body art removed, especially when celebrity couples break up and want the tattooed name of their ex taken off their body. From Johnny Depp and Winona Ryder to Tom Arnold and Roseanne Barr, spotlighting celebrity tattoo removal could be a unique way for a plastic surgeon to talk about a painful subject.

Industry-Specific Tips: Article Ideas

Finance and insurance: How to insure your home, how to tell if you need more insurance, and how to protect your family against the inevitable.

Real estate: How to boost the value of your house, all about mortgages, how to buy a house with no money down.

Manufacturing and wholesale trade: Current style trends, what to expect this season, what's new in fabrics, hot colors, new scents.

Administrative and support: The hiring of temporary help, why outsource your company's benefit programs.

Accommodations: How to pack a suitcase, off-the-beaten path attractions, historical sites in your area.

Healthcare: How vitamins and supplements interact with prescription medications, the importance of regular checkups, health advice for all ages.

How to Create a Tips Article for a Gourmet Food Store

The articles on your website should provide visitors with valuable information. For example, if you own a gourmet food store, you could offer a tip sheet titled "Double the Life of Your Fresh Produce." Throughout your article, be sure to include links to any products you sell through your online catalog. First, introduce the problem.

It's a well-known fact that the body doesn't store vitamin C, an important nutrient found in many fruits and vegetables. That's why it is necessary to eat fresh produce every day; unfortunately, most of us are too busy to make frequent visits to the grocery store.

Next, offer a solution to the problem you've presented. For example, you could simply list some tips.

Here's how to prolong the life of your produce and preserve its vitamin C content:

1. It's best to store produce unwashed and uncut in the refrigerator.

2. Once washed, separate lettuce leaves from the core and wrap the separated leaves in damp paper towels and place in the crisper drawer.

3. Once cut, store produce in plastic bags.

4. [Continue to provide tips.]

Next, you could offer another list telling your customers what *not* to do.

Avoid these common mistakes:

1. Don't store unripe fruits in the refrigerator—leave them on the counter until they reach the ripeness that you want, and then store in a cooler place.

2. Don't store produce on the regular shelves of your refrigerator. Place them in the drawers specifically designed for fruits and vegetables.

3. Some fruits, such as bananas and avocados, start to turn brown once they've been cut open. If you will be using only a portion of the fruit, cut it with a ceramic knife [make the words ceramic knife *a link to the product in your online catalog] to prevent oxidation.*

End your article by reminding visitors who you are. Add your marketing message, mission statement, or concept statement; and be sure to include your store location and contact information plus links to your online catalog.

XYZ Fine Foods is the southeast's best purveyor of gourmet foods and gifts. We're open seven days a week in ten locations in the South. Or shop online *[make the words* shop online *a link to your catalog] at your convenience.*

Your articles page functions as a repository or archive to showcase your expertise. Organize this page by using category headings so visitors will know where to find the information they need. For example a financial analyst could write headings for retirement planning, paying for college, information for home owners, and financial tips for small businesses. Then she would place the corresponding linked article titles under those headings. When a visitor clicks on an article title either a new web page or a PDF appears with that article.

If you offer a specific article as an incentive to get your visitors' e-mail addresses, tie it into the next level of product or service related to the free offering. Whatever you're offering as the giveaway should not be available on your articles page. The giveaway should be a stand-alone information product, unique and value-packed.

ARTICLE RESOURCE BOX

One of the most important aspects of writing an article is including a resource box that tells who you are and encourages readers to reprint your informational articles or link to them. For example, at the end of each article you could place a box offering reprint permission, such as:

> Would you like to reprint this article in your newsletter or on your website? You can as long as you keep the full attribution at the end.

> The following article can be reprinted provided you keep the resource box intact at the end. Please do not change this article in any way.

> If you would like to use this article, be sure to print my name, copyright notice, and contact information in its entirety at the end.

Article distribution protocol ensures that users must use your resource box. A resource box is simply an attribution with links. Here's how Joe Nunziata, a worldwide speaker, uses an effective promotional resource box:

> Joe Nunziata is an internationally known speaker and author of *Spiritual Selling*. He has been delivering his life-changing message since 1992. Joe has been studying the areas of personal development and human potential for more than twenty-five years. His unique blend of psychology, philosophy, spirituality, and the power of energy is designed to foster new attitudes in business and in life. Find out more about Joe and get your FREE CD and e-book (a $67 value) at www .spiritualselling.com.

If you cannot come up with an idea or don't have the time to write your own article, consult an article bank to find an appropriate piece for your website.

Submit to Article Banks to Increase Promotion

While writing articles is necessary for a quality website and e-zine, the real payoff comes in distributing those same articles to article banks on the Internet. An article bank is a repository for written material on every subject: business, health, work-life balance, and family, to name a few. Whatever your article's topic, you will find a category for submission. When you add your articles to a specific category, prospects anywhere in the world can retrieve your work and use it *with your byline*, which should include your name and contact information. Whenever someone uses your article, they *must* include the byline. The result is worldwide visibility and credibility. Your articles offer a powerful means to increase your database; readers who learn about you will click to your website for more information.

You can also use your own e-zine as a way to increase the readership of your articles. After your byline and copyright information, give permission to your readers to forward your e-zine and to share your articles; you've tapped into another way to spread the word about your business.

Article banks are essential in promoting visibility. One of the main advantages is that this free service helps raise your search engine rankings. Another advantage is that people from all over the globe gain access to your articles, and you build your reputation as an expert. Be sure to adhere to the specifications for each article bank. Some may require you to limit the number of links. Others may request a specific word count and mandate the amount of words per line. Three of the most popular article banks are found at these websites: www.ezinearticles.com, www.ideamarketers.com, and www.articlecity.com.

A short cut to submitting articles one by one is to submit your articles to a large volume of article banks at one time. For this you'll have to pay a fee and use a service, such as Article Banks (www.articlebanks.com) or SubmitYOUR-Article (www.submityourarticle.com), to submit your articles to hundreds of article banks at once. This saves time so you can focus on writing more articles and running your business.

Linking Strategies

The number of links to your site is a major factor that search engines consider when ranking your website. So the more people who link to you, the better;

however, you want to look at the quality of those links, not just quantity. *Quality* in this sense means sites that deliver your target audience to your own website. Such websites should be reputable, complementary, and not your competitors' sites. It's important that the sites you link to maintain a certain standard of quality. Anything less will reflect badly on you. Also be careful of endorsing only affiliate links (products that you sell for other people and for which you receive a commission). Your customers will not trust your recommendations and will think that you're just trying to sell them something, regardless of whether or not the product is of value.

If possible, use a company's logo as a hyperlink to its site. It's also a good idea to add a brief blurb about the company to which you are linking.

The big advantage of linking to other websites is that it can bring additional traffic to your site. If you are a pet sitter, you would want to trade links with pet shops, veterinarians, pet grooming salons, and pet food stores but not with other pet sitters.

Determine the types of sites that could potentially trade links with you. Focus on the sites related to your target audience. If you have a number of links, create a separate links page on your website. A good place to start your linking campaign is through a search engine like Google (www.google.com), Yahoo! (www.yahoo.com), or Open Directory (www.dmoz.org). Sites listed in these directories usually have high rankings from most search engines. After you find potential link partners, organize the information in a spreadsheet. The headings for the columns could be *keywords* (search words); *owner* (business owner or webmaster), *URL* (web address), *comments* (why you want to link to the site), and *date* (of initial contact).

Next, send a personal e-mail to each potential link partner. Make it easy for them to say yes! From your comments section in your spreadsheet, mention something you like about their site and why they should link to your site. Provide them with a sample link and explain exactly where on your site you'll place their link. It's easy as that.

Here's a hypothetical example of how to make the request in an e-mail:

Dear Mr. Jarvis,

I enjoyed my visit on your very comprehensive website. My name is Kevin Quinn, and I am the community outreach director for Books for Kids, a non-profit organization. Because we serve the same audience but don't compete, I propose we exchange links. We have a growing partner page with many of the biggest names in the area. Here's where I'll place your link: www.yourdomain .com/partner. My URL is www.yourdomain.com.

Please let me know by March 5 if this is agreeable. I know my customers would love to know more about your product.

All the best,

Kevin Quinn

Community Outreach Director

Books for Kids

Be sure to thank the people who agree to link with you and offer to send a copy of your logo to use on their site. Some people will not respond to your initial e-mail. After a few weeks, you can send out a follow-up note to encourage them to link to you.

E-mail Series Promotion (Autoresponder)

Using e-mail in a smart way allows you to connect with all your customers around the globe. This does not diminish the sincerity or authenticity of your communication. This is how it works: First create a series of e-mail letters that will be sent automatically after someone purchases a product or service from your website. When customers purchase your product, send an e-mail thanking them. Seven days later, follow-up with another letter asking your customers if they have any questions or need further information. Some time later, send a third e-mail that offers tips on how to maximize the use of your product or service, including innovative ways your product can be of benefit.

A month later you can provide your customers with a complimentary article based on their needs. Two months later, you could send out information about a related product. The goal here is to anticipate the needs of your customer and provide service and information at every possible level. On the one-year anniversary of your customer's purchase, you can offer an anniversary gift or special discount. The key is to create several touch points and solidify the connection with your customer.

One of new media's strongest features is sustaining relationships with customers and prospects. Using new media products is cost and time effective. Think of how many employees would be needed to touch base with the thousands of potential prospects and clients in your database. Through new media, you can let your autoresponder take over that task, saving time and money. But it all starts with you. *You* decide how often you need to connect with your customers. The technology is the vehicle, but you are the driver. You can subscribe to a dedicated autoresponder service to help put your e-mails on autopilot; two such companies are Aweber (www.aweber.com) and GetResponse (www.getresponse.com).

Your website is the foundation for everything you do online. If you create a website that authentically communicates who you are and what your business offers, and it makes a difference in the lives of your customers, you'll create a vibrant site that attracts your target audience.

How to Say It on Your Website

- Make it easy for customers to find you. Select a domain name that's the same as your business name or your slogan. Make sure you are listed on all the major search engines.

- Refine your home page copy. It is the first impression of your company. Have finely honed content that speaks directly to your target audience.

- Write conversationally. Use words to convey a feeling of warmth, professionalism, and trustworthiness.

- Choose the right colors. Your website should use colors that are industry appropriate and convey the tone you want to communicate.

- Use the correct pronoun. If you're a sole proprietor use the pronoun *I*, which is more personal than the pronoun *we*.

- Communicate your credibility. Build trust by posting your photo and biography and sharing testimonials.

- Build your client database. Include a lead-generating tool to capture visitor information when they browse your site, such as an opt-in box, sign-up box, or assessment tool. Encourage repeat visits by offering valuable information.

- Offer incentives. Create a coupon, and offer it as a free download to visitors who provide their name and e-mail address. Entice customers with a one-time-only discount.

- Use language that positions you as an expert. Convey your experience and expertise in a short statement.

- Focus on benefits and results. Create a message to attract attention to the value of your product.

- Use a variety of promotional methods. Engage in both Internet and traditional marketing strategies to promote your business.

How *Not* to Say It on Your Website

- Don't use corporate speak. Too much jargon can obscure your meaning. Be clear and specific in what you say.

- Don't use passive language.

- Don't focus on your own gains. Avoid phrases that emphasize greed and what you will get out of the transaction. Keep your focus on the customer.

- Don't lose track of the customer. Keep the emphasis on how you can be of service.

- Don't use multiple animations on your home page. If you must use animation, use only one and make sure that it highlights something important.

- Don't slow your site down. Avoid a long-loading Flash page that keeps your potential customers waiting. Visitors may click away before they even see the first word on your home page!

Part Three

Getting Your Message Across… With an E-zine

FIVE

E-ZINE ESSENTIALS

While your website is your new media foundation, your e-zines (or online newsletters) go out into the Internet universe, lasso your customers' interest and bring them back to your site. An e-zine is a regularly scheduled e-mail communication that entices your customers, informs them of your current offerings, and reconnects your business to their basic needs.

Marketing studies indicate that potential customers or clients need to hear your message at least seven times before they make a decision to buy. Consistently sending prospects your e-zine will help build trust and brand awareness so you can be the person who comes to mind when they need your service or products. Publishing your e-zine at least once or twice per month on the same date will give the strongest results. Choose a schedule and stick with it so your subscribers get used to receiving your e-zine. Weekly e-zines are great but take more time. Whether you are a business that deals mostly in B2C (business to customers) or in B2B (business to business), you can create a valuable e-zine.

Your website and your e-zine should work hand in hand. Think of your website as a relatively static series of pages that live on the Internet. Your e-zine, on the other hand, is periodically delivered in your customers' inbox offering them valuable information, perhaps an article or a tip, and definitely something to help them improve their lives or their business. E-zines also give you a chance to provide the latest news and insights on industry trends, updates on your business (whether it's promotions or any new feature), and any other timely information that you might not want to include as a permanent fixture on your website.

A good e-zine includes links to your website so customers can follow up and learn more about your business. Your customers should be encouraged to forward your e-zines to others, and so subscription information should be included in each issue. Your goal is to make your e-zine so compelling that readers look forward to receiving it and then forward it to their friends and colleagues.

E-zines also are a key way to build community and keep in touch with customers. Reaching out and growing your community becomes a cinch when you use an approach that connects all your new media components together. With the links embedded in your e-zine, you compel your audience to visit your website, post their thoughts on your blog, or listen to your latest podcast. Your community members will want to know what's new, what's different, and what you and your business are up to.

According to a 2008 "Marketing and Media" survey[5] conducted by Datran Media Research, 81 percent of industry leaders surveyed said that they will use e-mail to send online newsletters in their targeted e-mail campaigns. This approach by large companies has already trickled down to small businesses, which are using it to make a major impact.

Keep in mind, a key time-saving goal is to use your e-zine to market to your existing customers. These are the people who already know about you and your product and have shown, with their purchases, that they are likely to purchase from you again.

Marketing with any media is never static; on the contrary, it's dynamic and ever-changing. Your e-zine can be as simple as a text e-mail with a few lines about a change in your store hours or a new product or service, or as elaborate as a few articles to solve your customers' problems or even a video postcard to announce a sale. As a key brand extender, e-zines are your main tool for reaching your customers wherever they are. The Datran survey found that e-mail marketing lifts brand awareness by 58.4 percent.

More businesses plan to spend more money on this important tool as they recognize how it impacts their bottom line. The aforementioned Datran survey found that 67 percent of those surveyed believed that those e-mails have boosted sales through other channels. This is the key reason businesses using e-zines must know what to say and how to say it to make their newsletter stand out from the crowd.

Creating Symmetry among Your New Media Products

E-zines, blogs, and podcasts are the a la carte selections of new media products that enhance your foundation—your website. For these tools to be most effective, you need to think of them collectively when considering a name for them and creating themes to entwine them together.

Naming Strategies for Your E-zine

Shakespeare asked, "What's in a name?" For you and your business, the answer is everything. Your e-zine's name needs to connect to your business and your brand. When you name your e-zine, also mention a benefit—don't just call it "Free Newsletter." Make it specific and memorable.

Think about how you want your readers to perceive your business. In the scientific and technical trade, the qualities of thoroughness and precision are the most desired elements. In the construction and manufacturing industries, strength, durability, and timeliness are leading factors. The finance and insurance industries rely on accuracy, whereas the accommodation and food service industries rely on health and safety. For artistic professions, ingenuity, creativity, and being on the leading edge of thought are important qualities.

Consider what words or phrases invoke the professional image you desire. They can either be the actual words themselves or ones that allude to the desired image. When talking about health and safety, consider words such as *comfort* and *home*. When trying to relay the idea of timeliness, talk about meeting *deadlines* or being *deadline* conscious. Think of the word *exacting* when trying to convey thoroughness and precision.

Create a few phrases by putting together some keywords, and you'll see possible titles for your e-zine. Consider who will be reading your e-mail. A name that may resonate with industry insiders may mean nothing to your retail customers.

Industry-Specific Tips: E-zine Names

Real estate: A business that focuses on hard-to-sell properties could call its e-zine "Last Chance Help for Homes." An agency that focuses on foreclosures could call its e-zine "Half-Priced Homes."

Administrative: A typing service named both their business and their e-zine "Type-4-You."

Food services: A chocolatier who focuses on a variety of domestic and imported chocolates calls his e-zine "Sweet Treats."

An entrepreneur we worked with wanted his company to project a professional image targeting healthcare employees. He wanted his customers to know he was the resource they were looking for to help them overcome workplace issues in a healthcare environment. He recognized the most important words to convey these ideas are *balance*, *healthcare*, and *professional*. Ultimately, he chose a name for his e-zine that was a sum of all these values: "Balancing Act Solutions for Health Care Professionals."

Retailing specialist Bag Borrow or Steal (www.bagborrowsteal.com) tapped into the celebrity-fueled craze of designer bags. Their rental service offers fashionistas designer originals, such as Louis Vuitton, Gucci, and Prada, for a monthly fee. They use their e-zine (titled "Bag Borrow or Steal") to keep connected to their target audience, offering celebrity photos and the latest available styles.

Remember to consider your audience's typical age range and other demographics. For example, if you're catering to teens or young adults, you'd probably want to make sure you have a healthy dose of personality in your content and name. If you're targeting other business owners and/or professionals, it is better to concentrate on practical matters than on wit, although it's always important to present some level of personality in all that you do online.

How to Say It in the Basic Elements of an E-zine

The standard elements of every e-zine, or the *content formula*, must include your business information, a personal greeting, a value section, product information (ideally related to your value section), links for more information (embedded throughout your e-zine) that lead you to your website, privacy information, and subscription information (how customers can opt-in or opt-out of your mailing list).

Business Information

The business information in your e-zine should include your logo, your business's name, and contact information—including phone, e-mail address, website URL, and physical address. When you use an e-zine provider, you will be prompted to place this information in your template.

Your design elements are equally important. If you have created a header for your website, resize it so that you can use the same one for your e-zine. This will keep your branding consistent. If you don't have a header, consider some design element even if it's a bar of color that matches your logo. Starting out with only a plain white background with black text can be stark and clinical. Only businesses who want to set a very specific tone should use plain white. And even then, consider using fonts that create contrast.

When choosing your template for your e-zine, choose colors that are similar to your logo and the colors used on your website. The goal here is branding consistency. Think of Target. When you see the red-and-white bull's-eye, there's only one company you think of. That's what *you* are striving for.

Personal Greeting

The greeting area is your opportunity to speak directly to your customer. Keep it relevant but offer an emotional appeal. Even if you outsource your e-zine, as the owner you should be writing this section. You can't fake authenticity. Talk about something that is important to you this month, a challenge you have faced and how you moved past it, or something from your personal life that is relevant to your audience. You can talk about your business and what new services or products you are introducing or that are particularly helpful in this season.

An accountant can talk about new online processing for tax returns any time from January through April. A butcher could talk about how college basketball's premier tournament season, March Madness, inspires him to get together with his buddies and grill great rib eyes. The accompanying value section might include a recipe for a terrific dry rub to tie into the greeting. This is your chance to let down your guard a bit and let customers see the real you. Get creative. Think like your customer. What would you want to know? Organic marketing requires open and honest communication.

Value Section

The value section is the heart of your e-zine and should be the magnet that draws your customers back for more. Your goal here is to offer information that benefits your readers—saving them time or money, offering them insight, or opening a door to possibilities they had never before imagined. Providing this information will position you as an expert in your field.

No matter what form you use—articles, Q&As, or book reviews—keep your topics narrow and focused. Any component of the value section should be no more than 350 to 500 words. For all parts of the value section, include only the first few sentences or the first paragraph, then add a link to your website (usually titled "read more") to direct your readers to the entire article. You don't want to fill your e-zine with so much information that it is seems overwhelming. The full article can be housed on the articles page of your website. For more information on how to promote your business with articles see Part Two. Once readers are on your site, they can read through your archives or explore your site to learn more about your product, services, and business. This type of link allows the e-zine and website to work together smoothly.

Some elements to consider as prime components of your value section include articles, profiles, questions and answers, reviews, interviews, articles written by others, and statistical information. You do not need to have all of these elements in every e-zine. Select one or two instead and rotate your choices to keep your e-zine fresh.

Articles

Articles are core elements of an e-zine. They must speak directly to your audience. When looking for subjects to write about list the most common challenges your customers face. What keeps them up at night? What will save them time and/or money? What inspires or uplifts them? Knowing your target audience is key.

Article Titles to Jump-Start Your Imagination

Ten Ways to _____

Top Seven Signs of _____

Five Rules to _____

The Seven Universal Laws of _____

Insider's Secrets to _____

Write a 350- to 500-word article on solving a key challenge that relates to both your customers and your business. For example, a tax accountant may write on the top ten ways to get a refund from the IRS. A real estate agent may provide tips on sprucing up your home before putting it on the market. A life coach may write about how executives can achieve a better balance between work and home. The idea is to offer value.

Conclude the article with your name, contact information, and your resource box.

Make the article titles compelling, as you may use them to inspire e-mail recipients to open your e-zine (see "Writing Irresistible E-mail Subject Headings" on page 87).

Customer Profiles

Every business owner has some favorite clients. They could be your favorites because they were your first clients or your best clients or perhaps they have an amazing life story. By profiling such customers you are increasing your audience by capturing theirs! You can be sure that these clients will forward your e-zine to their friends, family, and colleagues. This is a powerful way to build your community. When your clients spread the word about your services, your business is sure to benefit.

Businesses in the healthcare industry might consider profiling a patient who beats the odds. Those in the construction industry could profile other business leaders in related fields, such as timber or steel, who are willing to discuss financial forecasts for the upcoming season.

An insurance agent might write about his city's businesswoman of the year, focusing on issues related to insurance (such as natural disasters or crime). In the article he should also mention that the honored businesswoman has been one of his clients for two decades.

Questions and Answers

In your e-zine, as well as on your website, in your blog, and in your podcasts, ask your customers to send in questions about the challenges or problems they face. You can then select one question to feature each month in your e-zine. This is a great way to engage your readers.

Businesses in the accommodation industry might talk about how to find hidden deals. A small business in the retail industry could answer questions about how a personal shopper can help out a busy executive. A religious institution could focus on a question they commonly hear from parishioners. For example, a church put out an e-zine that asked their congregation to submit questions for an author who is a parishioner and who credits his faith for keeping him grounded during his meteoric rise to success. The question he decided to answer was *How has your faith sustained you during periods of difficulty?*

Book Reviews

Many people love books. The problem is finding the time to read them and finding the right one to read. As a value to your customer, you can recommend books or resources that relate to your topic and industry. Consider becoming an affiliate with a bookseller, such as Barnes & Noble, or Amazon. Somewhere in your book review provide a link to the point of purchase; when your customers click through you may be able to receive a commission.

Florist: Flower Confidential: The Good, The Bad and The Beautiful by Amy Stewart

Real estate: The Western Guide to Feng Shui by Terah Kathryn Collins

Performing arts: The Artist's Way by Julia Cameron; or *Kate: The Woman Who Was Hepburn* by William J. Mann

A nonprofit group for filmmakers suggested reading the screenwriting classic *The Writer's Journey: Mythic Structure for Writers* by Christopher Vogler as required reading for all movie and documentary makers. They wrote in their e-zine, "It's what we're reading this month! Buy the book by clicking here."

Interviews

Readers enjoy reading interviews, especially when they focus on people with an interesting story. This can be a strong alternative to writing an article. The key is to find a compelling person whom your readers want to hear from. Ask questions that directly deal with what readers want to know about. One suggestion for connecting with high-profile experts directly is to visit the potential interviewee's website and look for contact information for someone in the communications or marketing department. Send an e-mail introducing yourself and your business. Then ask more than three questions and tell your contact that you'd like to use the answers in your e-zine. Many times publicity professionals will compile an FAQ that you will be able to use. The goal here is to think outside the box and make your value section truly impressive.

For example, when domestic doyenne Martha Stewart came out with *Martha Stewart's Homekeeping Handbook*—an encyclopedic account of everything you could ever want to know about cleaning and caring for your home—her publicist put together an eight-page document with questions and answers. This list could then be used by anyone who wanted to discuss and promote Stewart's book. The key is to realize that anything is possible and anyone can be contacted.

Guest Columnists

Consider asking an expert or respected colleague to write something for your e-zine. The benefits are that you get to present a new voice to your clients and offer new value. Look for someone who has something interesting to offer your target audience but who is not a competitor. Your e-zine may be the perfect vehicle for someone who has a podcast but no print media.

Industry Information and Statistics

Forecasting information can often be interesting, especially when the people receiving it would not normally be privy to it. For example, every year a company who studies trends in textiles comes out with their forecasts of the new hot color. Sending out information like this to retailing customers whets their appetite for whatever is new and trendy.

If you have a unique way of interpreting information and can provide evidence to back up your theory, present your ideas in the value section of your e-zine. For example, a restaurant owner could look into forecasts for high-definition television sales and perhaps examine the correlation of TV sales to restaurant take-out orders. The restaurant owner could interpret these data to mean that consumers are taking up a new interest in nesting, which includes in-home dining. In her e-zine article, the restauranteur could discuss how those in the food services industry could take advantage of this trend by increasing their take-out or delivery services or by creating frozen gourmet meals.

PRODUCT AND SERVICE INFORMATION

The best approach for the section on your products or services is the soft sell. Ideally, you want to feature a product that is related to an issue you addressed in the value section of your e-zine. You want your e-zine to become a seamless conversation rather than a haberdashery of information tidbits.

Feature a picture and a compelling write-up that focuses on the benefits your product will deliver. Be succinct. Use powerful verbs that convey action. You can call it a featured product, a seasonal special, or a new product or service. Each e-zine should feature a different product or service or at least a different aspect of your services; do not feature the same product more than once every three months, unless the product has been updated or expanded.

As with the value section, offer a link that will lead readers directly to a web page with more information about the product, along with an easy way to purchase it. You want as few distractions as possible between the e-zine and the purchase page on your website.

Offer the best-quality and highest-resolution photo of your product that you can without increasing the download time of your e-zine. The best format for photos is jpg or gif, and keep them less than 100 kb. Customers will be annoyed if their e-mail server becomes bogged down with large files.

You can showcase a product with a simple photo; if you offer a service, consider using a photo of someone successfully engaging in your service. If you are a doctor, show yourself interacting with or listening to a patient. If you sell homes, show yourself in front of a sold sign. If you run a temp business, feature one of your administrative assistants in a professional setting. Use every opportunity to highlight how well you have met your clients' needs. Your existing customers often provide a better and more authentic backdrop than do traditional stock images, which are available on the Internet for free. Note that stock photos can have a negative effect if your e-zine readers recognize the image from another vendors' promotions. Strive for uniqueness.

You can list a product once but no more than twice in the current issue. The first time should come directly after the value section. You can then mention it again, without the photo, before your closing or good-bye statement. Listing a product more than that is a hard-sell, which will turn readers off.

Remember, one of your goals is to stay alert to your customers' preferences. The tone here should be friendly and subtle, not over the top or in your face.

PRIVACY AND SUBSCRIPTION INFORMATION

Privacy is a serious issue in Internet marketing. All businesses using an e-zine must provide privacy information as a standard offering or else the e-zine could be considered spam. Your readers won't feel comfortable unless they know you are committed to protecting their information. As a business owner, you need to know that it's not always a bad idea to share information. Businesses that serve the same target customers can share information because they know that their customers can benefit. For example, a store that sells athletic footwear can share its list with a manufacturer of athletic apparel. An orthodontist might want to share her list with a tutoring service because both interact with middle-schoolers.

Many companies will ask website visitors if it's okay to share information with other businesses that offer products that are complementary with what they offer. The key is to give your visitors options. All good e-zine providers allow you to customize privacy information.

At the top of every issue of your e-zine should be a discreet message reminding recipients that they are receiving your newsletter because they requested to be on your list. Provide an easy mechanism or link for opting-out of your mailing list.

Selecting Themes

Having a theme will lend cohesiveness to your e-zine and will make it easy to read and easy to write. It's also a key time-saving strategy. Once you know the theme for the month's e-zine, you'll be able to narrow down information that relates to it.

You can create themes for an entire year so you won't ever have to worry about what to write about each month. When you have the time, you can create several different themes, and write your issues early, and then set them up to be delivered to your subscribers automatically each month. You can also bite off smaller chunks by planning out three months ahead.

Once you have your themes you'll be able to plug them into your content formula. For example, Betsy, a real estate broker, has planned three issues of her e-zine. The table below shows how she would say it.

Betsy's three-month example gives you an idea of how streamlined your e-zine production can become. The e-zine is made up of the same four sections (the content formula) each month. Whatever you choose as your formula for each section, keep it the same from month to month; only the theme and approach change. Each section should be broad enough so that the content can vary—that is, your feature could be an interview, an article you wrote, or an article written by another expert.

BETSY'S E-ZINE: THREE-MONTH PLAN

Month	Theme	Related Content Formula
January	Winterizing the home for maximum salability	*Greeting:* Chat about how January is the month for nesting and cocooning ▪ *Offer:* Complimentary market analysis ▪ *Feature:* Interview an expert about home winterizing ▪ *Recommended:* Resources on winterizing materials
February	Clutter control	*Greeting:* Chat about how clutter nixed a home's salability ▪ *Offer:* Free seminar or teleclass on what buyers see when they enter your home ▪ *Feature:* From Internet article bank: "Steps to Decluttering Your Home" ▪ *Recommended:* Book or video on clutter control
March	Landscaping	*Greeting:* Chat about showing a home with a flower-lined walkway ▪ *Offer:* Partner with a horticulturist to put on a free seminar at a flower shop ▪ *Feature:* Q&A with the horticulturist ▪ *Recommended:* Video on how to plan a flower bed; list of local landscapers

Tailor your themes to cater to a specific problem your readers can relate to each month. You may decide that a seasonal approach works best. For example, businesses in the retail clothing trade will want to offer themes tied to buying clothing for Easter in the spring, vacation wear in the summer, back-to-school clothing in September, and holiday clothing in the late fall.

A travel agent could match the themes of his e-zine to his clients' favorite vacation spots for each month. In January, because most people have usually had a busy holiday season, he could feature day trips or weekend getaways. In February, he could offer Caribbean deals. In March, he could focus on trips to Ireland to coincide with St. Patrick's Day.

Another alternative is to create one overarching theme for the year and use twelve months to break the goals down into bite-size nuggets. Mel Miller is a financial consultant who has many different aspects of her business that she can rely on to provide information for subscribers to her e-zine. One December, she brainstormed a number of themes for the upcoming year. She decided to go with getting your financial house in order for the new year.

In January, she gave a big-picture view of all the things that her subscribers needed to do to become fiscally sound for the year. Over the following six months she elaborated on each of the different components she mentioned in her January e-zine (for example, inventorying possessions, budgeting, credit cards, and investing in stocks and bonds and mutual funds). Each month she focused on one specific smaller theme that provided value in her e-zine. To read more about Miller, visit www.gcgwm.com.

The owner of a business in the wholesale trading industry whose customers are other wholesalers could choose an overall theme such as how to maximize exports. The first month, he could discuss how to identify foreign markets interested in his product. The next month he could talk about how to take advantage of currency fluctuations. The month after that he could talk about minimizing shipping costs by grouping them with other wholesalers.

Other Ways to Brainstorm Themes

Brainstorming is an active process. To get started, read and then read some more in your field. Find out what other people in your industry are doing. Subscribe to their newsletters. You may find that you could put a different spin on what someone else has to say. Or their ideas could spark new ideas for you. Keep an idea folder; when you come across articles that are relevant to your subscribers file them away. You'd be surprised at how this can be an ongoing source for valuable material. Once you've gathered a list of themes, select the ones that feel most appropriate for your customer base and that you are enthusiastic about. Your enthusiasm will come through in your content and will keep your readers engaged.

If something happens in your industry that's totally unrelated to the theme of the month and you want to write an article about it, consider including a sidebar or a brief note to alert readers to check your blog for more information.

If you're stumped for ideas try typing keywords in your favorite Internet search engine. A great tool is Google Alerts (www.google.com/alerts). This free service monitors the web and sends you daily information and tracks stories based on the keywords or phrases that you enter.

Technology Essentials

An e-zine is efficient and cost-effective because it is powered by e-mail. Jupiter Research found that targeted e-mail campaigns generate nine times more revenue than traditional broadcast mailings.[6] With such staggering figures, you must ensure that your e-mail reaches your target audience—your potential or existing customers. The only way to do that is by using an e-zine service provider rather than your own e-mail to deliver your e-zine.

Because of the stringent rules on spamming, it's best to avoid using your personal e-mail address to deliver your e-zines. Many common e-mail providers, such as Yahoo! and AOL, block e-mail if a large number of messages with the same subject are sent from a single address (the servers see this as spam). If you're going to spend the time and effort to create an e-zine, you want to make sure that it's actually getting to your customers.

Using an e-zine service provider makes the best use of your time. It also keeps your brand consistent by offering tools to maintain a similar look and feel with your website and blog. An e-zine service provider also creates and maintains your database of subscribers as well as gives your e-zine the ability to be forwarded and an array of other possibilities. But not all providers are created equal. Start with the provider that hosts your existing website. That

A Word about Spam

Spam on the Internet does not refer to the canned meat product. The spam we're talking about is the type that shows up in your e-mail inbox. The Federal Trade Commission issued stringent guidelines in the CAN-SPAM Act, which prevent individuals and businesses from sending out unwanted solicitations. The law's main provisions ban false or misleading header information, which mean an e-mail's from, to, and routing information must include the original domain name and e-mail address. The e-mail subject line must accurately convey the subject matter of the message. The e-mail must have an opt-out method. The law gives you ten business days to stop sending e-mail to anyone who asks to be taken off your list. Last, commercial e-mail should be identified as an advertisement and include the sender's valid physical postal address.

Violating each of the provisions of the act is subject to a fine of more than $10,000. The sender of deceptive commercial e-mail is also subject to laws banning false of misleading advertising. You can see why it is critical that any e-mail you send must follow the law. Spam filters are set to recognize common words and phrases used in unsolicited e-mail. Some popular phrases are *reverse aging*, *hidden assets*, and *stop snoring*. For a comprehensive look at one of the Internet's best list of spam triggers, based on frequency, visit the website of Ralph Wilson, a well-known e-commerce consultant (www.wilsonweb.com/wmt8/spamfilter_phrases.htm).

company might bundle e-zine capabilities either in the base price for web hosting or for a small additional fee.

Choosing an E-zine Provider

A quality e-zine provider will offer a tool to create your publication, preferably one that is WYSWYG (what you see is what you get), a place to store images, and a convenient image editor. Your provider can create and store a database that handles your growing audience; track who is opening your e-zine and when; deliver according to the schedule you want; and capture subscribers and add them to your database. It also offers an option to create a text-only e-zine (an increasingly popular option). Here are a few providers worth exploring. They all offer the options just listed and are the industry's leaders.

> Constant Contact (www.constantcontact.com). Offers great templates, is relatively easy to use, and has a low monthly fee. This provider can be used by virtually any business and, for an additional fee, will create a unique template for your business.

> GetResponse (www.getresponse.com). Offers the ability to use graphics, spreadsheets, Word or PDF documents, and audio and video streaming. This provider is great for information-based businesses such as professional services, real estate, and healthcare, who can use the video capabilities for maximum affect.

> 1ShoppingCart (www.1shoppingcart.com). Offers a comprehensive e-commerce system that integrates e-zine capabilities into its suite of services. It is ideal for business owners such as booksellers, retailers, and many service professionals who sell information products. Readers will be able to click on the product in your e-zine and easily pay using a shopping cart.

Before you choose an e-zine service provider, it's best to visit its website and take a tour to see all the features and benefits the provider offers, or sign up for a trial run.

Core Essentials

An e-zine is a comprehensive tool that offers your prospects and customers information, a personal greeting, and a featured special wrapped up in a compelling package. What makes it an organic creative process is how you pull all the various elements of an e-zine together.

At the heart of a great e-zine is relevant content that makes it memorable and recognizable. Savvy readers scan e-zines to find out what will speak to them. Your publication should start with a subject line that sparks interest and continue to deliver intriguing information to your customers and prospects. It should end with a link that sends your customer to your website.

Writing Irresistible E-mail Subject Headings

An e-mail subject heading is the first thing that your readers will see in their inbox when you send your e-zine. The first aspect to consider in the subject line is your name. Decide whether you will use your personal name (Kay Lewis) or your business name (Lewis Enterprises Media and Marketing) in the sender's (from) line. Keep it consistent so your readers will know what to expect when they see that name in their inbox.

Extend that idea to the subject line of your e-mail. Consider using the name of your e-zine and consistently use it as the beginning of your subject line. When your readers see that in their e-mail inbox, they will instantly know that it is a vital e-mail they should open immediately.

What you choose for that subject heading should grab readers, make them say, "Yes, that's me!" or at least make them curious enough to want to click that mouse and open your e-zine.

Subject headings for your e-zine are not much different from the headlines that you post on your website. Try using the attention-grabbing headline of your feature article or fashion a headline from that issue's theme. Speak to your customers' pain so that they know you understand what their challenges are. Create headlines that reflect this, and they will want to open your e-zine immediately.

Your readers will use the headline to decide if your e-mail should be opened now, later, or never. First and foremost, stress the benefits received from reading your publication. It should solve a problem and offer a benefit.

For example, an accountant who picked the name "Small Business Tax Tips" for his e-zine creates different subject lines each month, keeping the name of the e-zine but changing the benefit. For example, in January the subject line might read, "Small Business Tax Tips: Filing Early to Save Money." In February, it could read: "Small Business Tax Tips: What the IRS Doesn't Want You to Know."

Phrases and Sentences to Use in Your Subject Headings

Five Mistakes that Consultants Make on Their Websites

Do You Want to Get More Clients?

Three Easy Ways to Solve _____

How to Know if You're Saving Enough for Retirement

You Can Change Your _____ Now!

Industry-Specific Tips: Subject Headings

Social assistance (homeless shelter): Making a Difference in a Child's Life; an e-zine calling for volunteers

Performing artist (karaoke bar): Sing, Sing-a-Song; an e-zine listing just-added music and special offers for subscribers

Manufacturing (tool and dye company): Nuts and Bolts: Capacity Levels Open for Piecework; an e-zine to keep clients interested

Measuring Effective Subject Headings

Most e-zine providers offer you detailed statistics that provide a whole host of information, including who opened your e-mail, what time he or she opened it, what links your readers clicked on, and if any readers forwarded the e-mail on to others. If you're testing out whether your subject line is working, keep an eye on your statistics. Watch what happens when you use certain subject headings versus others. And choose the ones that offer maximum results.

Creating Compelling Content

As you approach writing your e-zine keep in mind two important tenets for high quality: relevance and brevity. *Relevance* means that your content is specifically targeted to your readers and means something to them. *Brevity* means that instead of boring your readers with lengthy text, your information is succinct and quickly makes all the important points.

Your e-zine's length will depend on how much you have to say, how often you speak to your customers, and how much time you have to commit to your e-zine. If you send a bimonthly e-zine, it can be shorter than if you write monthly. Articles should not be longer than five hundred words, and the entire content should not be more than a thousand words given the short attention span of today's readers.

You don't have to be a professional writer to produce an e-zine. What counts is the quality of your content. If it terrifies you to write, then by all means hire a professional writer. But make sure that some of your own personality shines through in your e-zine. Customers are looking for an authentic,

Generate an E-zine Step by Step

1. Choose a name for your e-zine. The right name is crucial to reflect your business and extend your brand.

2. Think of themes relevant to your business to plug into your content formula.

3. Select an e-zine service provider. Determine what features you most need and pick a provider who can deliver.

4. Develop a framework. Draw a sketch of what your e-zine will look like, using a content formula. Try not to use more than five sections; a long table of contents may prove daunting to your readers.

5. Develop your content.

6. Input or capture names into your database. These names can come from your website's opt-in box. Your e-zine service provider should have tools and wizards for setting up your database.

7. Distribute your e-zine.

organic experience, and that can happen only when you make your writing personal. But don't write about anything too personal. Your goal is to be friendly and accessible without crossing the line. Don't write about your tattoo unless you are a tattoo artist. Stay professional and on point. Your e-zine is an opportunity to build your best brand: You. Don't worry yourself with trying to create slick marketing prose because savvy customers have become immune to it all and will click away.

Additional E-zine Elements

In addition to the basic elements already discussed, there are a number of ways you can jazz up your e-zine. Don't think of writing your e-zine as a humorless exercise.

In fact, the way you approach creating your publication will translate to how your audience relates to it. You are not simply providing information; your goals are to get your customers thinking about your business and to widen their parameters. Sometimes you can accomplish your goals with humor or an inspirational quote. Other times it could be a startling statistic. Additional elements allow your e-zine to be well rounded. You might not know exactly what will grab your readers' attention. It might be the quote that keeps you in their thoughts. If you've entered their thoughts, you've accomplished what you set out to do with your e-zine.

To diversify your e-zine every month, you might want to consider rotating a variety of elements, such as an area for reader feedback, quotations from customers, or a pertinent statistic related to your industry. Or you could include factual statements if they are brief and relevant. Local and regional manufacturing businesses could include reader feedback about the resurgence of local mills. Or a personal development coach who encourages self-determination could include the Dr. Seuss quote, "Be who you are and say what you feel because those who mind don't matter and those who matter don't mind."

Another way to add relevant content is to ask a noncompeting business that shares the same target audience for some information or promotional material. You can also charge them a small fee for doing so or agree to do an information swap so they agree to include information about your business or product in their next e-zine.

Video and Audio Elements

The latest trend in e-zines is the integration of video and audio elements. The use of these elements should be judicious. An unexpected video or audio stream that is not relevant can be jarring and intrusive. For audio, keep the sound file short and make sure whatever is said is punchy and attention grabbing. For example, if you interview an expert for your value section and he says something revealing such as, "In the next five years, the industry is going to completely reinvent itself," that's powerful. Program the audio to play as someone clicks on the link. Then make sure the article enclosed explains or backs this up. The audio clip can also be used to link to a longer audio file or podcast hosted on your website.

Some industries can use audio more efficiently than others. If you're in the music industry, offer a ten-second snippet of a song with a link to your site where readers can hear more. You must also offer a way to turn the audio off or else it can be annoying.

Streaming video has become very popular, as well. Use it only if you have great, captivating images. Standing in front of the camera for thirty seconds is not compelling. If you're in the manufacturing industry and you've come up with a new way to package a product, a thirty-second video picturing the process could be enticing. A baker could show a speeded-up video of how to ice a wedding cake. A clothing boutique could do before and after shots of a makeover.

Consider using software that will help you compress your audio and video file so your e-zine will download quickly. Remember, both audio and visual elements should correlate to the value section and product information offered in your e-zine.

End your e-zine with a sincere and authentic closing. Use phrases such as *See you soon*, *Contact us if you have any questions*, and *Let us know how we can help you*. If your industry has a specific phrase that's used often, feel free to adopt it. You can be cute but avoid being kitschy. The goal here is to be authentic and approachable. You might also want to include a word about what topics your next e-zine will include so readers can anticipate it.

Plain Text or HTML?

Many e-zines are powered by providers and written in HTML (a mark-up language that allows for a variety of fonts and effects). However, there are a few reasons to consider distributing your e-zine in plain text (without images or design elements). Customers may be inundated with slick and glossy e-zines. A simple, paired-down approach can make you stand out from the crowd. Text

Plain Text E-zine Template: Any Business

E-zine Title

~~~~~~~~~~~~~~~~~~~~

Date [--/--/----]

From: [Your Name, Company Name, and contact information]

Privacy information: This e-zine was sent to you because you subscribed on our website or you gave permission by submitting your e-mail address. Should you want to cancel or change your e-mail subscription or recommend this newsletter to someone else, see the instructions at the end of this e-mail.

==

WHAT'S IN THIS ISSUE?

* Personal Greeting

* [Title of Special Offer]

* [Title of Feature Article]

* [Title of Special Resources or Recommendations]

==

Dear [Subscriber's Name],

Welcome to another issue of [E-zine Title]. [Greeting or welcome message.]

Inside this issue you'll find [summary of features and offers].

Sincerely,

[Your Name]

==

Title of Special Offer

~~~~~~~~~~~~~~~~~~~~

[Write-up of the special offer with link to website for more information]

==

[TITLE OF FEATURE ARTICLE]

By [Name of Author]

~~~~~~~~~~~~~~~~~~~~

[Include first few sentences or first paragraph of article with a "read more" link to website for the complete article.]

Article © 200[X]. [Your Name]. All rights reserved.

= =

[TITLE OF SPECIAL RESOURCES OR RECOMMENDATIONS]

~~~~~~~~~~~~~~~~~~~~

Check out this new book: [Title of Book with "order here" link to point of purchase]. [Include first few sentences or first paragraph of review with a "read more" link to website for the complete review.]

= =

Like this e-zine? Please forward it to an associate or colleague who you think will benefit from this information.

~~~~~~~~~~~~~~~~~~~~

© 200[X]. [Your Name]. We never rent or sell subscriber lists to any third party. Your privacy is very important to us.

To subscribe to this newsletter, [insert "click here" hyperlink]. You may unsubscribe by sending a blank e-mail to: unsubscribe@[yourdomain].com

HTML E-zine Template: Historical Romance Author

Historical romance author Robin specializes in the Regency Era. She has published her first novel and plans more books. She quite rightly considers her writing books to be a business. So she sets out to attract more readers and sell more books by publishing an e-zine. She develops a simple content formula, which includes a table of contents with links:

Greeting
What's new
What I'm listening to on my iPod
Feature section

GREETING
[Professional photos of her and her upcoming book]

Dear [Customer Name],

I'm so excited to send you my first e-zine! Because you're an avid Regency reader, I'd like to tell you that my new book will be released in the next few months. It's a scintillating story that I'm sure you'll love.

Right now, I'm gazing out the window of my writing studio and my backyard is buried in virgin snow—like a Currier and Ives lithograph. The utter beauty and tranquility should inspire calm, but all hell's breaking loose inside the house— dishes piled in the sink, mounds of ironing, burnt roast—as I race to meet the deadline for my next Regency novel. Shhh, it's a secret. But you, my subscribers, will be the first to know when this new novel is ready to hit the shelves.

Not everything is a secret though. In this e-zine I share an excerpt from my latest book so enjoy! I've also started a contest, just click on the link to enter. I hope you win!

Sincerely,

Robin

WHAT'S NEW

WIN THIS! Five lucky winners will receive a signed copy of my latest novel, which *Vermont Reviews* called "sublime!" Visit my website to learn more.

WHAT I'M LISTENING TO ON MY IPOD

I've discovered NPR's *Echoes*, which airs on Sunday nights from 7 to midnight. I went straight to www.echoes.org and purchased the download for my iPod. I've been listening to the music all week while I write. It's that unobtrusive. It's the perfect background sound and doesn't interfere with my brain waves.

FEATURE

Here's an excerpt from my new book:

Chapter One

At midnight, when she saw him, Lady Elyse Fraser fled the stuffy ballroom to her bedchamber. She now sat on the floor—with legs tucked beneath her beautiful, voluminous gown. She stared vacantly at the small cluster of paintings depicting a hunting scene, but couldn't find the fox.

Miriam burst through the bedroom door without knocking.

Elyse jumped, her fingers reaching for her throat. "Oh it's you."

Read more…

To preorder the book, click here.

Next month's e-zine will bring you the latest in my new Regency series.

Happy Reading,

Robin

Click here to change your subscription settings or to unsubscribe. Click here to forward this e-zine to a friend.

© 200[X] RR Books. All rights reserved. 1234 Main Street, AnyCity, AnyState 11111, USA

www.[Robin'sdomain].com

---

e-zines offer stripped-down content with lower risk for being detected as spam. And with the proliferation of PDAs and other mobile devices, text e-zines are far easier to read.

E-zine service providers give you the option to convert your HTML newsletter into plain text, so sending in either format won't be any additional work. If you're concerned only with content and are confident that your readers won't care about aesthetics, then plain text e-zines might be right for you. See the boxes on pages 93 and 94 for examples of e-zine templates in both forms. Many e-zines use full-color templates with all the bells and whistles. If you want to create one for your business, then HTML is the way to go.

Alternatives to an E-zine

While crafting an e-zine is the way to go, there are alternatives. You might consider sending an online postcard, which is like a small flier compared to an e-zine's letter-like appearance. Postcards should primarily be used to drive sales or a specific event. For maximum impact, postcards should have a great photo, a headline, and a link to your website for more information.

You can also use an autoresponder to send out notices or letters to your customers at specified intervals. These are usually used after a sale to touch base with your customers and to find out if they need additional information. You could create an e-book that is divided into twelve parts and send one segment every month automatically.

The goal is to keep your business in the forefront of your customers' minds. But one of the most effective ways to consistently do this is with an e-zine.

SIX

TELLING YOUR AUDIENCE ABOUT YOUR E-ZINE

Getting your e-zine ready to go is just one part of the equation. The next crucial part in launching your e-zine is finding a ready audience. If you have already defined your target audience as suggested previously, an e-zine is a tremendous outreach tool that will extend your brand and build your community. A list of all your prospects and clients/customers in one place—your database—is a valuable asset. And the size of your customer database can greatly determine the success of your e-zine.

Who Is Going to Read Your E-zine?

Start with your existing customers and add anyone who might be a potential customer. You'll already be capturing e-mail addresses through your website's opt-in box (or boxes). If you don't have anyone on your list yet or not as many names as you'd like, get out your address book, your cell phone directory, your PDA (personal digital assistant) contact directory, and your e-mail address book. Comb these lists for potential names and e-mail addresses that you can add to your database. Send each person an informal introductory or grassroots e-mail letter about your company (see Chapter 11 for more information). In that same e-mail, you can give readers the option of unsubscribing from your e-mail list by replying to you with such a request. Then you can safely add all those who do not opt-out to your database without the risk of spamming them. After you've exhausted these possibilities, the next step is to start a campaign to grow your database.

Immediately Increase Your Database

An authentic list is crucial for establishing your community. This type of list is composed of people who want to hear from you, respond to you, and—ultimately—buy from you. This is not a list that you pay for, and it doesn't consist of arbitrary people who have no vested interest in your business. A list of voluntary subscribers results in greater responsiveness and interaction. An audience that wants to hear what you have to say will read your e-zine.

Think about joining some professional associations; you may then have access to the membership database. Check out each organization's privacy policy and the rules governing the use of members' personal information. In some cases, you may have to ask the organization to forward your introductory e-mail to its members. Once the organization sends out your e-mail to its membership, potential customers who like what they read will opt-in to be on your list. This is a great opportunity to increase your database and build that all-important authentic list.

Another way to increase your authentic list is to collaborate with other businesses or organizations that serve the same audience. For example, the owner of a bed and breakfast approaches her town's travel and tourism department and volunteers to write an article for the department's website about great places to visit in their city. At the end of the article, the B&B owner should include a link to her website and an opt-in box for her own e-zine. This creates a win-win situation all around. The tourist department gets a free article, interested prospects opt-in to receive more information about the area, and the bed and breakfast owner expands her marketing database.

You can also consider creating strategic partnerships to create an e-zine that will serve not just your own business but also other related businesses. For example, a small group practice of general practitioners can approach other local healthcare professionals who share the same target audience—such as registered dieticians and physical therapists—to create an e-zine focused on healthy eating, exercising, and preventative medical care. All three businesses can pool the names of their patients for the broadest distribution of their e-zine.

Industry-Specific Tips: Strategic Partnerships

Lawyers and financial consultant: E-zine targeting entrepreneurs with a focus on legal and financial issues all business owners should know

Makeup artist, hairstylist, and clothing store owner: E-zine targeting young professionals with a focus on monthly makeovers

Restaurant and a wine shop: E-zine targeting gourmet cooks with a focus on phenomenal wine and food pairings

Caterer, event planner, and wedding gown designer: E-zine targeting prospective brides with a focus on how to prepare for the big day

Increase Your E-zine's Open Rate

Even if you have used a double opt-in method to create your subscriber list, you are not home free. According to a white paper by Merkle,[7] a marketing database agency, research shows that most people open and read only approximately sixteen permission-based e-zines that they receive.

The key is to create such value that your e-zine is in the top tier of the publications your subscribers open. An e-zine is the quintessential e-mail marketing tool that you can use to consistently build your core community.

A Successful Strategic Partnership

Wellness Coalition America
www.wellnesscoalition.com

When national fitness expert Terrie Reeves and seasoned television producer Kay Jones Lewis joined forces, no one could have predicted that their union would affect the health and wellness of so many people.

Armed with just a few hundred names in their joint Rolodex files, the pair started an e-zine with the goal of sharing cutting-edge and relevant information with the public. They invited experts in the health and wellness fields to contribute columns and write tips for their monthly e-zine, which became the focal point of the organization whose mission is to be a trusted resource for health information. The pair brainstormed and realized that if their e-zine were to grow, it would have to meet the needs of two distinct groups: people who were looking for quality local health information and small business owners who wanted to provide some additional value to their customers but didn't have the time, energy, or know-how to produce their own newsletters.

Reeves and Lewis persuaded local and regional healthcare experts to forward the e-zine to others, and the idea paid off for them big-time. Soon owners of sports stores, health-food supermarkets, and vitamin distributors were forwarding the Wellness Coalition America's newsletter to their customers. Within a year, more than forty thousand people were reading the monthly e-zine.

Promoting Your E-zine

Even though you may offer a free information download on your website to attract subscribers in exchange for their e-mail addresses, it is customary to bundle the freebie with an e-zine.

It's not enough to say, "Sign up for my free e-zine." You need to provide a fifteen- to thirty-word description of exactly what your subscribers will get by signing up for your publication and filling in the opt-in box on your website. Your description should clearly convey the benefits the reader will get by subscribing. It also helps to communicate who you are, so let your personality shine.

Industry-Specific Tips: Descriptions for a Monthly E-zine

Professional services (life coach): Articles, tips and insights to help you live a balanced life

Retailer trade (small store owner): Subscribe and get the latest fashion alerts—find out what's hot and what's not

Healthcare (fitness trainer): An e-zine to support you in achieving your best weight

Don't forget to say it with pictures. Because an e-zine is an intangible product, an image will help ground it. With so much information on a web page, it makes sense to create an eye-catching representation of your e-zine to attract attention. Make the image of your e-zine look like a magazine cover, keeping in mind your website's overall color scheme, look, and feel. A cover gives a higher perceived value than just text. Also, think about how much the information you're sharing every month would cost. Give it a monetary value. For example, a carpenter who charges $75 an hour and writes an e-zine on handy tips for the home could say, "$75 value."

You can design your own cover using an image-enhancing program or ask a graphic designer to create one for you. You can also check out www.killer-covers.com for a professional-looking e-zine cover at a reasonable cost. Place the cover image near your opt-in box on your website.

Attract Prospects with E-zine Directories

An e-zine directory will house your e-zine and can be a gold mine for attracting your target audience. By submitting your e-zine to a directory you expand your reach beyond your own database. Businesses who recognize that your service would enhance their client base could forward your e-zine to their audience

If you want to find e-zines that serve your similar target market but are not your competitors, then an e-zine directory is your best bet. You can explore the directory to locate complementary e-zines and determine whether you want to buy, sell, or swap advertising; exchange articles; or find a strategic partner. A strategic partner can promote your offerings to his mailing list or you could team up to offer a teleseminar or virtual seminar. You are only limited by your imagination. The opportunities are enormous for your business, including more subscribers and tons of traffic to your website.

Directories offer every category, including business and finance and healthcare. You can post a paragraph that describes your e-zine and intended audience and, depending on the directory, you may be able to add more specific information. For the industry leaders, visit these sites: The Directory of Ezines (www.directoryofezines.com), Ezinelocater (www.ezinelocater.com), BestEzines (www.bestezines.com), and New-List (www.ezine-universe.com).

When you register with an e-zine directory, it will request a short blurb about your e-zine. In your write-up, include information about your company, your marketing message, and your contact information. Most important, stress what your e-zine offers and its target audience.

How to Say It with E-zines

- Pick a theme for each month. After determining your theme, introduce it and then provide a relevant solution or address a need related to that theme.

- Write conversationally. Use words that you'd normally say out loud to engage your reader. Write in first person, using the pronoun *I* instead of *we*, *they*, *he*, or *she*.

- Address your readers by name. Use your subscriber's name in the greeting section of your e-zine.

- Mention your personal life. Add some personality to your publication by mentioning your dog, cat, or children; a recent vacation; or milestone event. Offer just enough information to become a real person to your readers, without going too far.

- Proofread your work. Be sure to use correct grammar and punctuation; even if you run a spell checking program, you must still proofread everything you write to ensure a level of professionalism.

- Write relevant content. Whether you present an interview, an analysis about an industry trend, study findings, tips, or how-to's, make sure that the content is focused on your target audience.

- Use graphics. Add a relevant image or two to enhance your copy.

- Create an attention-getting subject line. Remember that your subject line must compel readers to open your e-zine.

- Practice the soft sell. When discussing products or services, use a soft-sell approach.

- Assemble an authentic list of subscribers. Make sure that your subscribers have opted-in and that you are not sending spam.

- Distribute your e-zine to your target audience. Although your subscriber list comes from your own database, seek opportunities to expand your readership.

How *Not* to Say It with E-zines

- Don't use a generic greeting. Avoid starting your e-zine with something like "Dear home owner." Address each reader personally by the user-name they subscribed under.

- Don't create an e-zine that is radically different from your website. Your publication should have the look and feel of your other promotional materials.

- Don't use a free e-mail domain for distributing your e-zine. Not only is this unprofessional but you may be subjected to spam filters. Use a professional e-zine service provider and/or your own domain web-hosting tools.

- Don't write lengthy tomes. No one has the time to read a ton of information. Be brief.

- Don't offer only self-serving content. Although you want to promote your services and products, readers will be interested in information of value. If your publication does not provide a benefit, readers will unsubscribe.

Part Four

Getting Your Message Across... With a Blog

SEVEN

BLOG ESSENTIALS

Of all the new media components, blogs have had the biggest effect on the way businesses communicate with their customers. Blogs are the most direct two-way online communication vehicles, making them the heart of organic discourse. They're engaging; they're interactive; and as a result, they create a conversation, not a monologue.

Thanks to their informal tone, blogs can offer fresh insights into a company, allowing for direct access to decision makers and encouraging communication between customers and prospects.

Like all the other new media tools, a blog must have a specific target audience to be successful. This is the same audience you are targeting with all your online marketing efforts. New media components appeal to different learning styles. While some readers may love your e-zine, others may be drawn to your blog because of its informal tone and interactivity.

Your blog's focus has to be narrow and speak to a specific group to be effective. A blog that is too broad won't appeal to anyone, while a blog with a specific identity can take a narrow topic and discuss it in depth. This allows you to stand out from the crowd and further confirm that you are an expert in your field. For example, lunch boxes from the 1970s have become a rage. The items that once cost $4 now sell for hundreds and sometimes thousands. A business owner we worked with who deals exclusively with lunch boxes has expanded his business exponentially by blogging about these collectibles and attracting this core community.

Blogs are a key tool in building community. Customers, who would not normally have the opportunity to converse with one another, can use a blog to interact not only with you, the business owner, but also with each other. By being a catalyst for conversation, a business's blog becomes a virtual water cooler to attract like-minded people.

A 2006 Pew Internet and American Life Project survey found that blog creators have grown to about 12 million American adults...and that the number of blog readers has jumped to 57 million Americans.[8] Corporations such as Apple, Starbucks, and General Motors were the first to jump on the business-blogging bandwagon. Apple has incorporated user feedback into various generations of iPods. The leadership at General Motors collectively write a blog called "FastLane" (http://fastlane.gmblogs.com) where they discuss some of the latest products in GM's family of cars. But blogs are not just for big business. Nor are they exclusively for political diatribes and teenage rants. They're for any business that wants big results. Small- and medium-size businesses may be the ones that can best benefit from a blog's quality of intimate community building. Blogs foster the kind of communication their customers rarely have in offline life. Communication over the Internet allows for safe intimacy. Customers feel protected by the inherent anonymity offered by technology; and as a result, they tell you the truths they would not say to your face.

Many small businesses use blogs to keep on top of what their customers truly need and want. Think of it as your own market research. If you understand your customers' challenges and how and when they use your product and service, you position yourself and your business to be able to serve their needs. While you are responding to your customers' questions and comments in your blog you can offer your service or product as the ideal solution. Remember, however, that your approach must be subtle.

Before you begin expanding your product or service line, use your blog to test the idea with a receptive audience. If you think your product needs an upgrade, try asking leading questions in your blog; by your readers' responses, you'll know if you need to make changes. Your blog is the place to generate customer comments about how effectively your product or service is being used. Current customers will use your blog or their own to offer feedback on your existing products or services. When Microsoft launched their Vista operating system, software users all over the world rushed to blogs to talk about the benefits of and kinks in the software.

Blogs offer you a chance not only to listen to your customers but also to talk to them in an informal tone. One of the best aspects of blogs is that they are personality driven, allowing your target audience to see you as a real person instead of an anonymous business owner. On the other hand, retain your professionalism; you want to be approachable while maintaining your expert status.

The beauty of new media is that you can choose to create a blog but not an e-zine or even a website. Shocking! You can use as little or as much as you want. Be aware though that the level of results you receive is in direct proportion to the variety of new media tools you use as well as the level of your commitment. Using them all is a surefire way to maximize your results.

From a new media standpoint, blogs raise your search engine rankings; some blogs are more effective at this than their accompanying websites. *Spiders*, the automated programs that check out all the pages hosted on the World Wide Web, love blogs for the simple reason that these tools are constantly seeking new content. Blogs, by their very nature, are updated more frequently than websites.

For business owners, blogs could be the first step in creating an online presence for their products or services. Blogs are easier to update than normal websites. Many blog providers offer their software for free, which can be a boost for companies just starting out. These reasons make blogs ideal for any business that is dipping its toe into the new media universe.

What you don't spend in money, you need to put in with time to make your blog the most effective it can be. You will need to post to your blog at least twice a week—and more if you can—to reap the most rewards from blogging. Readers will come to rely on reading fresh content; so be sure to update your blog on a regular basis.

If You Build It They Will Come

Providing readers with relevant content and updating frequently are the keys to attracting an audience for your blog. Your posts don't have to be long. Even a few sentences can be enough. But get into a habit of producing regular posts so your readers know they can rely on you for pertinent information.

To create content that attracts a large readership, you'll have to consider a few critical points. Determine what your core audience craves. What kind of information would they consider valuable? How can you deliver it to them to make their lives easier or more interesting?

Once you can answer those questions, you'll begin to understand what kind of content you can provide.

Stirring the Pot—Attracting More Readers

Another component for making your blog unforgettable involves stepping out of your comfort zone. Tone is one of the leading ways to impart personality in a blog. Think about posting content that stimulates discussion. This is not the time to be a milquetoast. Sometimes, as in shock radio, you have to provoke and stimulate conversation. But don't spout opinions that are not your own. If you tend to hold back some of your stronger opinions because you are observing the rules of etiquette and don't want to turn anyone off, your blog is where you can remove the gloves. When you sanitize your comments to make them more palatable for a wider audience, you can sometimes lose what's important.

Remember, though, that the goal is to be interesting, not offensive. You want interaction, you want reaction, and you want people to comment. The best way to do that is to prod your readers and see what kind of reaction you get. Keep in mind that to keep and attract readers, your blog must provide some benefits or value. Think about ways in which you can stimulate conversations with and reactions from your audience.

Industry-Specific Tips: Stimulating Readers

1. Going Against the Tide

Technical services (information technology consultant): In a blog to small businesses: "The first-generation iPhone is dead. A device that cannot properly access remote servers and download your business e-mail does not meet all the needs of a working professional. I say, until the second-generation iPhone is developed, keep your BlackBerry close."

Real estate (agent in New York City): In a blog to newcomers: "Paying to live in a rat-infested apartment should not be just another adventure in city living. It's crazy to rate an apartment by the number of resident rats. Imagine calling your mother in Iowa and telling her that today you saw only one rat in your home! Everyone deserves to live in a clean abode. And, believe it or not, there are places in the city that are rodent free. I invite your comments."

2. Being Cheeky

Retail trade (independent bookstore owner): In a blog to readers of popular fiction: "J. K. Rowling's last book in the Harry Potter series reads like a Dan Brown novel. Its suspenseful beginning and climactic ending makes *Harry Potter and the Deathly Hallows* stand out from the others in the bestselling series. Rowling clearly saved the best for last. Your thoughts?"

Artists (portrait painter): In a blog to art historians: "Pointillism was the worst thing that could have happened to the art world. Realism is the only thing that matters. Everything else is imagination at its worst."

Offer Insight

Television writer Bob Harris wrote such a detailed explanation of the last episode of *The Sopranos* that his blog (at www.bobharris.com) was visited by more than two hundred thousand of the show's fans immediately after the show's last episode aired. His popularity spread like a virus because readers loved his insights and forwarded the link to his blog to others. You can be certain that if he decides to continue his deeply interesting analytical approach to other shows, people will read his blog. Harris will be remembered and perhaps hired in the television industry because he explained something that left so many viewers scratching their heads. He offered value to his readers while increasing his own name recognition.

Ultimately, what makes a blog memorable is relevancy and personality. Bloggers who offer a unique or individual take on an interesting issue will be able to attract readers. Blogs encourage personal interaction like no other new media tool.

Creating Symmetry among Your New Media Products

Throughout this book, we have talked about the importance of symmetry among your new media outreach tools—website, e-zine, blog, and podcasts. Whatever you have decided to name your business, website, or e-zine, you need to extend that same idea to your blog and all your new media components to create cohesive branding. There are a number of different ways you can approach naming your blog. Consider creating a single online name and putting the word *e-zine blog* or *podcast* at the end to identify the medium. Or use your business name in the same manner.

Another option is to create a stand-alone name. Take a look at your marketing message: What word or phrase can you extract to use as a blog title? Because your message is based on the benefits you offer, use a key value—time, money, or experience—you offer and use a variation of it as the name of your blog. Keep in mind that in the world of the web, size matters. Your blog name should not be too long, and the URL should fit easily in a web browser's search box. It can be frustrating for your readers to type in a long web address that uses non-standard spelling,

If you have a cookie business, then the word *cookie* should be somewhere in the name of your blog. If you have a tattoo shop, the word *tattoo* or *tats* should be in the name of your blog. Your blog title should reflect what your business is about. If you have a pet store named Pet Supplies Unlimited and your dog Shakespeare sleeps by the register, don't name your blog "Shakespeare's Puppy Patrol." It's too oblique. No one would get it because Shakespeare is not universally identified with pets. However, if the name of your pet business actually is Shakespeare's Puppy Patrol, then you can name your blog "Shakespeare's Puppy Patrol Blog."

A secondary component to consider is the inclusion of a subtitle, which expands on the name. For example, if you choose your business name as your blog, you can use a subtitle to broadcast what you will be blogging about. You also can incorporate your personality into the subtitle. For example, a well-known tattoo artist may use the following subtitle: "Snake's Take on Asian-Inspired Tattoos." A reader may remember the blogger (Snake) rather than the topic. This takes your business communication to the next step, to a more personal level. Readers may search for the blogger or the business owner's name, rather than the blog title. Think too about the keywords a potential customer is likely to type into a search engine.

Remember, your blog's title makes a statement about who you are and identifies what you do. It has to be short and memorable.

Industry-Specific Tips: Naming Your Blog

Reviewer (books): "Bookgasm: Reading to Get Excited About" (www .bookgasm.com); goal = recognizable name that is not dramatically different from the business's name; don't create customer confusion.

Wholesaler trade (church accessories): "Sacred Objects: The Blog"; goal = reinforces the brand and purpose of the products; don't cheapen the business by using a blog title like "Terrific Tchotzkes."

Artist (wildlife photographer): "Ian Shive Photography" at www.waterand sky.com; goal = name recognition with a URL that reflects the content of the photos.

To Theme or Not to Theme

In Part Three, we discussed the importance of developing themes for all your new media components. This can save you time and help you focus when you're writing your new media content. It will also create a cohesive set of online publications.

By *themes*, we mean having a monthly plan of what you are going to talk about that correlates to what matters most to your customers. You could have a theme for each month or you could use a seasonal theme that would run for two or three months. For example, November and December are holiday months during which you could use a general holiday theme. A life coach could use "relax, renew, reinvigorate" as the theme for these months.

August and September is the back-to-school season. Booksellers, office-supply stores, clothing stores, and others could tap into this idea during the late summer.

Choosing a theme for a month's content requires you to think broadly. Before you choose a theme, ask yourself if there is enough content for at least eight to twelve posts (assuming you are blogging two or three times a week, four weeks a month).

Should you prefer not to use themes, there are a variety of approaches you can take. For example, your clients are interested in issues related to your business; you can post a blog entry that introduces updates to your products and services. Because the newest and latest information is always valuable—no matter what your industry—consider blogging during a visit to an industry trade show. Your readers will love the cutting-edge information they won't be able to find anywhere else.

You can use news events that relate to your business, or take some aspect of pop culture and tie it into what your business offers. A financial analyst could blog about the effect the president's state of the union address will have on the stock market. A psychologist could blog about an actor's recent breakdown and the signs and symptoms that everyone should be aware of.

Offer your opinion on a business-related topic and link to other blogs that are talking about the same topic. You can analyze industry trends, write a book review, or conduct an interview with another professional. It all comes back to value and what your customers want. The point is to make your blog interactive and engaging.

By using the same theme for all of your new media components, you will be able to integrate your marketing materials while working efficiently. When you use the same theme for each component during a given month, you save research and preparation time and you don't have to worry about what to write. For example, if a gardening service's theme for October is spring-blooming bulbs, the e-zine would offer articles on how to choose and plant bulbs; the podcast would be an interview with a horticulturist about bulbs for the local agricultural zone; and the blog would invite gardeners to share their experiences with bulbs and to post photos of their flowers.

Technology Essentials

Blogging involves more than just writing. An effective blog site includes video, audio, photos, a subscriber box, an RSS feed, and a unique header (a graphic image that sits at the top of every blog page). These elements combine to create an aesthetically pleasing online environment for your customers and prospects.

Choosing the Right Blog Provider

Most blog providers offer a series of templates to help you create your blog. For a consistent look and feel, choose colors that match your offline and other online marketing promotional materials. There are numerous blog services out there. What most business owners don't know is that you can set up a free blog within five minutes. But if you want all the bells and whistles, there are plenty of options, too. Check with your web hosting service or try one of the following well-known blog providers.

WORDPRESS.ORG

WordPress.org (www.wordpress.org) is arguably the most sophisticated and flexible business blogging software available, but it has a learning curve. You have to fiddle with some technicalities, including backing up and upgrading your blog when there's a new version of the software. To start using this blogging software, you have to download it to your computer and find a host. Your best bet is to use your website provider so all your hosting is done under one roof. BlueHost (www.bluehost.com), a full-featured web hosting provider, is one of the best hosts for WordPress blogs because it offers an automatic installation that quickly integrates your blog.

WordPress.org also offers a vast number of free plug-ins (cool features to trick out and enhance your blog), themes, and templates to help ramp up your blog. You can also purchase a template to make your blog unique. Best of all, WordPress is free.

Here are some things to consider before choosing WordPress: If you set up your blog through your own website, the URL to your blog will include your domain name, which boosts your branding efforts. Those who are tech newbies should know that although WordPress provides documentation and hosts user groups and forums, it provides no direct support for its users. That said, WordPress is a solid choice if you are comfortable using a little HTML code and installing plug-ins.

WORDPRESS.COM

WordPress.com (www.wordpress.com) is also free and is easier to use than its big sister, WordPress.org. WordPress.com is a fully hosted blogging platform, which means that if you decide to set up a free blog hosted by WordPress.com, you won't need an independent blog host and you won't have to bother with the technical details, such as backing up, upgrading, and installing plug-ins. On the other hand, customization of your blog's look is limited; you can't change the background color or even all of the headers. Furthermore, you cannot use your own domain name in the URL unless you use domain mapping. If you set up your blog through WordPress.com, your blog's URL will end with www .yourblogname.wordpress.com.

A word of caution: WordPress.com will shut down any blog *hosted on its site* that is created for marketing or search engine optimization purposes. It does not permit advertisements. However, WordPress.com welcomes business professional service firms such as lawyers, accountants, stockbrokers, and Realtors, as well as a wide range of nonprofits. Before setting up a blog with any hosting service, be sure you read and understand the terms of service.

TYPEPAD

TypePad (www.typepad.com) is a professional blog provider that charges a monthly fee. With built-in enhancements and a wide range of professional looking templates, TypePad is easy to use and has emerged as a solid front runner for business blogging.

Some of the best features include the capability to mirror the look and feel of your website by using your site's exact colors and importing your website header. Selecting categories is also a strong feature as well as easy integration with external plug-ins to enhance your blog (including search boxes, polls, and other handy widgets). It's also the best choice if you want to integrate your blog with other social media sites such as Facebook—it puts your TypePad posts directly on Facebook.

A downside of TypePad is the excessive amount of spam that you may have to deal with—which is relatively nonexistent with WordPress. But if you want to set up your blog and go, without the back-end details, then TypePad could be the blogging platform for you.

MOVABLETYPE

Those business owners looking for the Cadillac of blog providers should consider MovableType (www.moveabletype.com). They power some of the most high-powered blogs on the Internet including NBC News and the Huffington Post. MovableType offers the ultimate in sophistication and is best for a business that wants to make a sizeable impact with their blog presentation.

MovableType is the most expensive blogging platform. The cost of using it is in proportion to the bells and whistles you require—and there is no trial period. Some of the downsides of choosing this platform are its difficulty in installation and its steep learning curve.

BLOGGER

Blogger (www.blogger.com) is free and powered by Google. It offers a variety of themes and makes it easy to set up your blog. Blogger's somewhat informal look and the lack of subject headings (categories) may not be right for all businesses. Businesses who have had the most success with Blogger are artists, writers, and those in creative fields.

Blog + Website = Blogsite

Extending further into the blog realm is a hybrid of a blog and website called a *blogsite*. A blogsite is similar to a website, but blog posts are made directly on the site's home page. There are advantages and disadvantages to setting up a blogsite. The advantages include having the convenience of a single web-based property. Instead of paying for the hosting of two sites, you pay for only one. This means you will market only one URL instead of two (one for your website and one for your blog).

If you own a business that will thrive on enhanced interaction, such as a service-based business, a blogsite might be perfect. It offers a place to post the fixed information of a website while allowing for the dynamic interaction of a blog.

Blogsites are not recommended for product-based businesses that need a online means to attract customers to product offerings such as a shopping cart for instant purchases. A blogsite's content is constantly changing. As a result, there is no static page to effectively drive home your marketing message.

If you want to sell information products and collect e-mail addresses, then consider setting up a website. If you are looking to spotlight your personality and vault your visibility or if you have a lot to say and are looking for a platform to espouse your views and opinions, then a blogsite may be just the medium.

Core Essentials

Your blog will bring you up close and personal with your readers more than any other new media tool. With it, you engage and interact with readers on a deep level, find out what's on their minds, and commit to a discourse on a regular basis. When you integrate these principles of organic small business into your blog, you are bound to convey the right tone.

The tone and length of your posts are two of the most important components to understand when blogging. The tone of a blog is informal and casual. The difference between the language on your website and that on your blog is akin to the difference between what you wear during the workweek and what you put on for casual Fridays. On casual Friday, work is still done and professionalism is still needed, but you have a chance to let your personal style shine.

To find the right tone for your blog, look at the language you use with your most frequent customers. You want to be open and friendly without being inappropriate. The language used in each industry differs. Generally, legal and financial sectors are more formal than retail and food-service businesses. Find the right balance by writing several posts and ask some of the people you know and trust for their reaction. You can sometimes get a general sense if your blog is hitting the mark by the comments you receive, both online and in person.

The length of a blog post is generally shorter than an article. Two to three paragraphs can suffice, as long as the information is specific and targeted. Your blog posts should be no more than 250 words. Anything longer can be broken into multiple posts. Bear in mind that online readers surf headlines and skim content. Keep your sentences short and punchy. Use active, muscular verbs.

Creating Compelling Content

What you say and how you say it are important for creating a blog that brings readers back day after day, week after week. A successful blog presents logically organized information. When you post frequently—as you should—you'll quickly amass a vast amount of data. You'll want to sort your blog content into easily identifiable and searchable components.

Categories

Categories are ways to organize your blog posts and represent the key areas of your blog's content. Categories are usually listed on the static area of your blog—to the left or right of the page or in a sidebar.

Like a book's table of contents, categories serve as navigational tools to help readers quickly find the information that interests them. Your blog's categories, however, are presented in a clickable format. If a reader wants to learn about a particular aspect of your focus topic, she simply clicks on the category of interest and all the content you have ever written on that specific subject will appear.

Limit the number of categories you plan to use; lots of categories may indicate that your blog is unfocused and too broad. It's best to create your categories when you initially set up your blog. If you need to add more categories as you post, then you can do so. When you have a niche and your topic is focused, you'll easily create enough categories to cover the content of your blog. Avoid filing too many posts under a heading such as "uncategorized." Only a desperate reader will search for information there. *Hint:* If your blog post doesn't fit into any category maybe it doesn't really belong on your blog.

Apart from serving as an organizational tool, categories offer the benefit of attracting more traffic because your blog will pop up when a prospective client conducts an Internet search using one of your categories as the keyword. Attracting tons of traffic through search engines can sometimes be a negative. If a reader clicks on one of your categories and finds only one or two posts that are a year old, your credibility is shot with that potential customer. This is another reason to keep your blog topic narrow and focused.

Industry-Specific Tips: Categorizing Your Blog Posts

Professional services (information technology specialist): Networking, computer repairs, troubleshooting, Microsoft, Apple, industry news/trends, software reviews, tools/gadgets

Medical industry (in-home nurse): Nursing shortage, nursing issues, nursing intrigue, surveys, home-care tips, medical career or medical jobs

Construction (architect): Design/aesthetics, environment, projects, fairs/conventions

Travel industry (independent agent): Caribbean, Europe, USA, vacation tips, news, favorite destinations, hotel reviews

If your blog hosting service does not offer a way for you to categorize your information, then find one that does. Logically categorized blog posts are a hallmark of any professional blog.

How to Say It: Blog Posts

Now that you've categorized your information, the next step is to write your blog posts. As always, the best thing to say in a blog post is something that offers value to your customer or client. This information can be news, a tip, a question-and-answer segment, an interview, a short article, an analysis, or anything that will make your customer's life better in some way. These are similar to the topics you may have used in your e-zine. That's okay. In your blog you will offer a different take or ask your readers to comment on something you have written in your e-zine.

As advised previously, when it's time to come up with a blog post, look to your theme for the month. If you wrote an article in your e-zine about how to lay tile, you may want to provide an FAQ in your blog to engage your customers. Invite readers to comment about your posts so you can create an ongoing conversation.

Relying on a monthly theme is the easy way to keep your new media publications up-to-date, without creating a time-sucking drain. Having a list of themes means you'll never be left without anything to write about.

On the other hand, when you have a flash of inspiration or want to talk about something timely, you can either write an extra blog post or substitute a new post for one of your themed posts.

SAMPLE BLOG POSTS

Professional Services

In February, at the height of tax season, an accountant chose tax guidelines as her theme. In each of her posts, she wrote a different tip. She started with

"Small Business Series, Tax Tip No. 1: Did You Know That Your High-Speed Internet Is Tax Deductible?"

> Thinking of turning in your dial-up connection for DSL or a cable modem? If you use the Internet primarily for your business you can deduct the cost of installation and the monthly fee as a cost of doing business.

Her next post was titled "Small Business Series, Tax Tip No. 2: Keeping Track of Auto Receipts."

> Keeping a brightly colored small folder in your glove compartment to collect your gas, parking, and toll receipts will help you sort out your deductions at the end of the year.

In July, her theme was about organizing tax information at the year's mid-point to keep from being overwhelmed in January. One of her blog posts that month was called: "What Are You Doing with Your Receipts?"

> You know you need to keep them but how do you keep them from being crumpled in the bottom of your bag or in a drawer? Streamline all your financial expenditures by using a money management program. Software like Quicken can help you keep track of what you spend. And here's an added bonus: The cost of the software is tax-deductible, too!

All of her blog posts are focused on a monthly theme and the core offering of her business: providing tax-saving advice.

Retailer

A florist decided not to have a set monthly theme but instead uses the calendar as a prompt for blog topics. One March, she posted a blog entry with this title: "What's Hot This Week!"

Are you ready for spring? Holland just sent in their most beautiful tulips. We have all the colors that will brighten up any drab March day!

In Holland, flower colors have meaning. Pink is for romance, yellow is for friendship, and white stands for purity. To supplement your soil, consider adding bone meal or any type of alkaline product to help preserve the true colors of your bulbs.

Hang in there, winter is almost over!

That July, the florist's posts focused on summer flowers. One was called "Vase of the Week."

Ancient Greek potters created approximately twenty different kinds of vases, which served functions such as carrying perfume for sacred ceremonies, cooling wine, and storing water. These days vases are not only decorative and fun but are functional. They also guide the shape of your floral arrangements.

When looking to display long-stem roses, consider a tall vase that fans out so that the buds are not crowded. Make sure to plant daffodils by themselves. The sap from the blooms is poisonous to other flowers. For those looking to display floribunda or grandiflora roses from your own garden, consider a round crystal ball to create English charm.

Our vase of the week is a 32-inch crystal vase with a sturdy bottom whose height is perfect for gladiolas, which are on special this week.

Her subtle plug for her business's product is incorporated into information that will help her customers know what flowers go with what style of vase.

Food Services

Steve runs a successful bakery in the Pacific Northwest. In his blog, "Baker's Dozen," he talks about what's in the oven each morning, the life of a baker, artisan flours, organic ingredients, and wine and bread pairings. Here's a post he titled "Another Op'nin', Another Show."

It's 4 a.m. and sometimes I truly feel like the guy who utters, "Time to make the donuts." But what is it that lures me out of my warm bed on a cold, dark morning? The chance to bake with a wonderful new flour that just came in from King Arthur. The organic wheat makes loafs light, fluffy, and nutty. I'm going to make a multigrain wheat bread with honey that always makes me drool.

In another post, titled "What Wine Goes with a Rosemary Loaf?" he wrote this:

How about a great glass of Malbec? The wonderful South American wine has notes of tobacco that stand up well to the piney taste of the rosemary. Add some creamy cheese such as Brie and you have yourself a meal! Enjoy!

The blog is as quirky as Steve is. The key is that his customers learn a great deal about the whole process of baking. This content entices them to return for more of his blog posts. He has earned a terrific following of customers, and blog readers now know him as "That Bread Guy."

His blog is a terrific example of how personality shines through a blog and can drive customers into your store. Don't be afraid to reveal who you are. Steve could expand on any of these blog posts and turn them into articles for an e-zine. Or, if he doesn't want to write an article, then he could offer a short recipe for chocolate chip cookies using King Arthur Flour. In the next post he could write a longer article or his musings on his favorite Malbec wine.

Responding to Blog Posts

Blogging is not just about creating a post and you're done. You need to remember to look for and respond to the comments your readers leave on your blog. Try to do this within twenty-four hours after a comment has been posted. Most blog hosting services will e-mail you every time someone leaves a comment.

Be sure to acknowledge what the person had to say, even if you don't agree with it.

For example, an owner of a shoe boutique that sells stylish shoes for fashion fanatics could blog about what's hot now. When she posts her list of the hot shoes for the season, her blog is read by thousands of shoe fans who visit her site.

The Shape of Things to Come!

This season, it's all shape inspired. Everything from the shape of a shoe's heel to the open-toe area is changing. The peep-toe shoe is getting a makeover with an almond-shaped opening. Platforms are getting a cone-shaped heel. And even flats, the favorite of last season, will see more embellishments with hardware. Will you be wearing the new shoes? What's your favorite shoe?

Posted by Helen, Sunday, 9:15 a.m.

COMMENTS

I love platforms! But why do I always think I'm going to break my ankle?

Posted by ShoeGrrl, Tuesday, 10:15 p.m.

ShoeGrrl, I feel your fear! I fell off my platforms in sixth grade and have avoided them ever since. You might want to try wedges. We have some great ones that give you the same lift without the fear. Or boots! This year, it's about a boot wardrobe and you get the same Emma Peel sauciness without the threat of a sprained ankle.

Posted by Helen, Wednesday, 2:30 p.m.

Through her comments, Helen was able to engage her customer while keeping the door of communication open. She also made a subtle plug for her store's other products. ShoeGrrl now feels there's a real person behind the blog to whom she can relate to—that's the start of a lasting customer–retailer relationship.

Unveiling Your Content with Tags

The elements that reveal what your posts are about are tags. These hyperlinked, relevant keywords work on the same principle as categories to describe the major content in your blog posts.

Your blog hosting service will likely provide a tag generator. If not, search for a plug-in that works with your blog software. A tag generator may create a tag cloud, which is a visual depiction of your content that is displayed in the static area of your blog—on the left or right panel. Tags are displayed in different sizes and colors to demonstrate how many times you've used the words in your blog posts. When your visitors click on a tag, they will be presented with links to all your posts that contain that word. This saves your readers time, helping them quickly locate specific content.

Industry-Specific Tips: Tagging Your Blog Posts

Wholesaler (fish monger): Blog that describes the catch of the day—salmon, whitefish, flounder, mackerel, tuna, grouper

Food services (coffee planter): Blog that discusses bean roasts—Arabica, Blue Mountain, java, Juan Valdez, Colombian, decaffeinated, full roast, French roast

Administrative (professional organizer): Blog with tips on how to keep your office clutter-free—sort, organize, discard, prioritize, bins, shelves

The most common tag clouds are user-generated and are based on frequency of use. The ones that are used most will appear in font sizes larger than the other words. These types of tags show you what words are being searched on within your site and are most popular throughout the blogosphere.

Tag, You're It!

Donald owns a bridal specialty salon. He uses his blog, "Bridemonster," to take a tongue-in-cheek stab at the crazy world of weddings and some of the brides he encounters. His blog is a lot more humorous than his website, which functions as the place where he talks about the lines of bridal dresses he carries, his shop hours, and so on. But his blog is so funny it ends up being the main source of traffic to his website.

Some of the tags on his blog are wedding, dresses, brides are crazy, bride monsters, bridezillas, dress dramas, wedding dresses, wedding dreams wedding nightmares, wedding dress dream, dream dress, dress meltdowns, brides and their family, brides and bridesmaids, brides cry, brides scream, brides and grooms, brides and no grooms, brides and churches, and brides and bridal party.

Content That Counts

An about us page is standard for most business blogs. Even though you will reveal a lot about yourself in your posts, your readers will want to know more details. Whet their appetite with background information that explains why you are qualified to write your blog; add contact information and a photograph.

If you want to be recognized as an industry expert or a thought leader in your industry then go one step further and use your about page as a press page. Include the following data: information about the company, including key personnel, statistics, demographics, and company history; press releases; information on public appearances and copies of speeches; a book excerpt or blurb; high- and low-resolution digital pictures of you and your company; FAQs; videos; and a professional biography that details your education and professional experience. When journalists conduct research on your topic, they'll find you as a resource and will want your information fast. So make it easy for others to download your information; this will set you apart from other sources.

Alternatively, you can include a link to an online press kit posted on your website or a link to your pressroom at Eworldwire (www.eworldwire.com). Eworldwire is a news release distribution service that provides members with a virtual newsroom.

Showing Other Facets

While categories, tags, and the about page solidly identify the business content of your blog, adding personal components to the sidebars can identify who you are and round out your personality. A link to a Flickr (www.flickr.com) photostream showing you and colleagues at an industry conference or even of you and your dog could help you bond with your readers. The benefit is that it shows your human side; just don't overdo it.

Incorporating a link to your Twitter (www.twitter.com) page can ramp up your bonding with readers. Twitter is a real-time broadcasting tool that asks you one question: "What Are You Doing Now?" You reply in 140 words or less. Your followers, or "Tweets," respond with what they are doing and so it goes. The sign-up is free and Twitter is simple to use. Its capabilities as a significant marketing tool are yet to be realized—but in the meantime, have fun!

EIGHT

TELLING YOUR AUDIENCE ABOUT YOUR BLOG

Once your blog is set up and you're posting regularly, the next step is to let the world know about it. It isn't enough to rely on search engines; you must practice blog-specific outreach methods that will maximize your blog's visibility. You should take a two-pronged approach to promoting your blog. The first part is technical. You need to ensure that your blog distribution tools are in place. Your blog service provider will offer tools such as a linking mechanism to create a blog roll as well as a means for readers to subscribe via e-mail or other automatic feed. The second part deals specifically with outreach and promotion. The goal is to reach your prospective audiences by being accessible. Make it easy for others to hear from you and make it easy for your readers to find you.

Make Use of Blog-Distribution Tools

Your blog hosting service provider—the host of your blogsite or website—offers tools for distributing your blog to a wide audience. Some providers allow you to enhance your blog and extend your reach by using plug-ins and third-party software. But at least some distribution tools come with your blog software, and these are enough to get you started in telling your audience about your blog, linking to others, and engaging your audience.

Using Blogrolls to Gain Readers

Linking is the lifeblood of the Internet. Being able to go from one new media tool to another with related content is one of the inherent strengths of these marketing devices. Listing links—to both blogs and websites—can serve your readers and help them connect to other information not only among your own new media sites but also on related sites. This list of links is called a *blogroll*. A blogroll is a set of links that are usually placed in a sidebar on the blog's main page. Depending on your business, you'll want to post links to community connections, sponsors, noncompeting peers, clients, and government resources.

When you add a blogroll you are not giving good business away. Yes, readers may click away from your site and never return, but the possibility is there for you to gain even more readers. You will also gain readers from other sites that include your link in their blogroll. In the end, it's a win-win situation for everyone. The best insurance for keeping readers coming back is to provide good, valuable content in your blog posts. Your goal is to serve your customers' needs. A successful relationship on the web is not built on a tightfisted approach. Like the infinite universe, the web is abundant in its resources, and there's enough for you to get your share.

In essence, by placing a blogroll on your blog you are showing your community affiliations. You're letting your readers know about the sites that are valuable to you and thus may be valuable to them, too. By linking to other bloggers, you are letting them know that their posts are valuable and may help your readers. A blogroll is one way to join the global blog community or blogosphere.

The first place you may want to check for blogroll links is the partners or links page you created on your website. Or examine your community pages to find other related businesses. Be sure to include links to any blog that has positive things to say about you, your business, or your blog.

If you've defined a niche for your products or services, look for other blogs or sites who are also servicing your target audience. Be a resource for your site's visitors. Recommend a trustworthy company on your blog. That company may reciprocate. This mutual exchange is a great way to treat your customers well and to become the go-to person when they have a problem or need.

Industry-Specific Tips: Blogrolls

Construction (door and window dealer): Links to window treatment businesses, interior designers

Accommodations (bed and breakfast owner): Links to car rental companies, airlines, tour companies

Retail trade (clothing store): Links to closet coordinators, image consultants, jewelry stores

Administrative (bookkeeper): Links to tax accountants, lawyers, office supply stores

By offering relevant content and being visible in the blog community, you will increase the chances that other bloggers will add you to their blogrolls. Use the blogroll tool that came with your software or consider a link-list manager such as BlogRolling (www.blogrolling.com). A blogroll tool allows readers to add your link to their site with a single click.

Adding blogs to your blogroll can be as informal as reading other blogs and selecting the ones your readers will like. Or it can be as formal as sending an e-mail invitation to bloggers whose sites you'd like to add to your blogroll. Doing this implies that there should be reciprocity.

A Homeowners' Association's Blog

BLOGROLL INVITATION TO BUSINESSES

In this example, a homeowner's association wishes to share links with local businesses.

> *Subject: Join Our Blog Community!*
> *A 500-home subdivision has a well-read blog that provides residents with an online site to share information, tips, and neighborhood news. We'd like to support our neighborhood retailers by featuring their website or blog links on our blogroll. Let us know if we could exchange links.*

BLOGROLL INVITATION TO RESIDENTS

In this example, a homeowner's association wants to exchange links with businesses owned by the development's residents.

> *Subject: Neighbors Helping Neighbors: Gain More Exposure for Your Business*
> *Our new blog is getting more and more popular. We love to encourage our residents to use each other's businesses. Please send us your blog or website link so we can add your business to our blogroll.*

For a community-oriented organization, sending out a mass e-mail to local vendors is fine. However, most individual business owners simply capture the link they want and add it to their blog roll.

Use Trackbacks to Gain Readers

A *trackback* is an acknowledgment tool that lets other bloggers know that you have mentioned them and are sharing their information with your readers.

If you let people know via a trackback that you discussed them in your blog, then quite possibly they will mention you too and maybe even send your link to their friends and associates. This is a great way to gain new readers.

Rather than posting a number of comments on several different blogs, trackbacks offer you the opportunity to keep your thoughts on your own blog while linking to others. Your blog hosting service can provide you with a trackback tool, so you can easily participate in the global blogging community.

Here's an example to show how trackbacking works. George, the owner of a local touring company, could post the following to his blog:

> The Smoky Mountains are beautiful during October, when the leaves change to yellow, rust, and ruby. According to a local bed and breakfast owner, "We have the best views of the foliage on this side of the Smokies." But a forest ranger we talked to last week said that she might be viewing her last fall foliage from the patio of the B&B. The county has decided to . . .

If George wants to let the B&B owner know that she's being discussed on his blog, he can go to her site and copy the URL (via a trackback link on the B&B blog, if there is one). George returns to his own blog and pastes the URL in the appropriate trackback box (sometimes labeled "URLs to Ping"). When the owner of the tour company saves his post and publishes his blog, the trackback software will notify the B&B owner, letting her know exactly what's been written about her.

While trackbacks work well to notify when someone is being discussed in cyberspace, it is best not to repeat verbatim what was said. It's not enough to just parrot someone. Include your own comment to add to the discussion. You may even spark a conversation back and forth between your blogs, which will be more dynamic and may interest even more blog readers to your posts.

Feed Your Readers with RSS

By far the most important blog-distribution tool is RSS (real simple syndication). This web-based software catches information from your blog and distributes it to readers who have subscribed to your feed. RSS gives your blog readers automatic access to your blog whenever you post something new.

Once a blog is set up with an RSS feed, you will see a small orange icon displayed on the blog's home page; the icon may also appear in your web browser's location bar, depending on what software you use. To subscribe to a blog's RSS feed, click on the icon. Once you've subscribed to a blog, you'll have access to all the new posts with just one mouse click.

If you set up an RSS feed for your blog, your readers will be able to subscribe and thus be instantly informed when you update your site. Subscribers use a variety of means to access their RSS feeds. Depending on the web browser they use, they may be able to click through to your blog through their browser's toolbar. Other subscribers may choose to use a news reader or feed reader (originally called an RSS aggregator). Examples of news readers are MyYahoo!, iGoogle, NewsGator, Sage, and Google Reader. Feed readers allow your customers to see all your new posts as soon as they are published; this keeps you in touch with your clients, even on days when they don't visit your blog directly.

According to a 2005 RSS usage statistic from the Pew Internet and American Life Project, "6 million Americans get news and information fed to them through RSS aggregators."[9] It's likely that these figures will continue to increase as feed readers become more mainstream.

Some industry analysts believe that RSS will eventually replace e-mail as the main way information is distributed. Feed readers are constantly looking for new information. That's why updating your blog frequently is critical. When your readers see that your blog has not been updated recently, they may choose to unsubscribe and turn to a blog that is more current.

Many business owners bypass the RSS supplied by their blog hosting service and opt instead for one of the most popular and highly recommended free services: FeedBurner (www.feedburner.com) or FeedBlitz (www.feedblitz.com). These services provide RSS feeds and enough features to blast your blog to the top of the blogosphere like nothing else. And most blog hosting services support and easily incorporate these products.

Along with delivering your blog posts to your readers' computers, these services offer powerful promotional and optimizing features and efficiently handle e-mail subscriptions to your blog. FeedBlitz has a free basic service and a paid service for more upgraded features, such as branding your feed. At the time of this writing, FeedBurner (owned by Google) offers all of its services for free and will deliver blogs via e-mail that has your company name in the from line. FeedBlitz, on the other hand, puts its own name in the from line. One of the keys to branding success is consistency. This seemingly simple feature of a custom "from" line could prevent your blog notification e-mail from being overlooked.

FeedBurner offers other promotional features, tag-generating tools and an animated banner that automatically highlights your three most recent posts. You can display this banner not only on your blog but also on your website, in your e-mail, on social networking sites, and in your e-zine. A banner is much more attractive than a simple link. If one of the headlines displayed in the banner strikes a chord, you have a new reader.

Both FeedBurner and FeedBlitz automatically notify the popular blog directories and search engines of your new posts. And they offer in-depth blog analytics—such as how many people visited your blog and the links they clicked on. No doubt RSS is a must-have feature for your blog, helping you reach the widest possible audience.

Gain Exposure with Your Blog

Once you've used all the blog-distribution tools offered through your blog provider, it's time to reach out on your own to explore the blogosphere.

Commenting and connecting with other bloggers is the first step. Listing your blog on blog directories so that you can be found is another step. Expanding your platform and becoming a guest blogger are more steps to gaining exposure for your blog and your business.

No Blog Is an Island: Commenting on Other Blogs

Your blog doesn't stand alone. It's in a sea of other blogs; and like islands connected by bridges, your blog is part of a vast web connected through hyperlinks. Tapping into this connectivity is crucial for the success of your blog and for building name recognition. But you must be willing to write comments on other blogs before expecting people to post on yours. Find blogs that are likely to be read by your target audience and start becoming a presence on these sites.

Even if you offer products and services to the same audience, these blog owners are your peers or recognized thought leaders. Don't be afraid to stray from your own backyard. You can even go on a competitor's blog, as long as you add to the conversation. Think of it as a natural extension of sharing information. It also goes without saying that when you comment on your competitor's blog, don't bash his or her business. Your intent is to expand the conversation and build a positive image of you and your business. But avoid blatant promotion for your products and services.

On your own blog, if you want people to post comments, end your posts with open-ended questions. Ask for feedback. This is the time to speak out. It's also a prime opportunity to interact with your customers.

EXAMPLE BLOG COMMENTS

Professional Services

Jane is the owner of a creative coaching company called the Coaching Creative. She left the following comment about a post published in a competing blog.

How Long Should You Wait Before You Self-Publish?

Now seriously folks, how many rejection letters would you collect before you go to Plan B? A friend of mine has kept all her rejection letters since 1988. And you'd think they would be discreetly tucked away in a carton box. No. She has papered the walls of her den with them, and she's still collecting. Personally, I would not want to enter my creative space every day and see those harbingers of doom that say: "Unfortunately, I don't feel this is what I'm looking for at this time, and I have to pass. But best of luck!" It's been 19 long years.... Self-publishing, anyone?

Posted by Sean at Publish or Die Coaching Services, Saturday, 1:00 p.m.

COMMENT

Hi Sean. Your friend's situation is indeed a conundrum. But one thing I have to say is she has faith in her writing. I have to applaud her tenacity, too. So many people seek validation from external sources—whether their work is good enough or whether they are good enough, etc. She has found what she loves to do, and apparently if she gets published, great. If not, these "harbingers of doom" remind her of her journey, and she stays the course. Should she self-publish? As experienced professionals, we know that this is an entirely subjective decision, and she has to find her own answer. I say trust your friend to know when her cup is full.

Posted by Jane, The Coaching Creative, Saturday, 6:00 p.m.

Community Organization

John is the president of a Little League team. One the most popular blogs read by his target audience is F.I.T. Outreach, a community lifestyle blog run by fitness trainers. Here's how he responded to a recent post:

How Are We Going to Solve the Teen Obesity Problem?

The number of teens who are overweight is alarming; our schools need to do more to address this problem. Because of the recent mentality of teaching to the test, most kids have classes all day and don't have time for P.E. Then they come home and sit on the couch. What are we going to do to motivate the youth of our community to start exercising?

Posted by F.I.T. Outreach, Tuesday, 3:10 p.m.

F.I.T. Outreach, you do a great job of providing tips for helping kids to get more active. We all need to get involved. Whether it's organizing walks a couple of days a week in our subdivisions, or making Saturday a walk-only day in our community, let's get some ideas flowing what we can do to help.

Posted by Little League, Tuesday, 5:30 p.m.

By offering suggestions, building on the original post, and presenting some solutions, John has made some valuable contributions to the blog. He also raised awareness about his Little League organization in the signature line.

Attracting Subscribers by Listing in Blog Directories

Letting the world know where and how to find your blog is smart marketing. In addition to being listed in the databases of search engines, blogs are rated by popularity in blog banks. Such banks are also a great place to view what else is out there in the blogosphere.

The top places to submit your blog and to search for other blogs are Technorati (www.technorati.com), Google Blog Search (blogsearch.google.com), Blogarama (www.blogarama.com), and BlogPulse (www.blogpulse.com). These blog directories categorize blogs by topic. For example, if you want a blog that deals with health, you can surf just that category. Submit your blog to these free directories to make sure you show up when a potential client begins to search for information on your topic.

Expanding Your Platform

Blogs can help connect you to other businesses in your industry like no other new media product. Creating a blog that broadens the scope of your business opens the door to other opportunities. If you provide a service, don't just look at your own business, look at your entire industry. Determine what type of businesses you could blog with. A carpenter might consider teaming with a garden store to discuss making decks for the backyard. A car detailer could create a blog with several car dealerships and highlight a different make and model in each post.

Instead of blogging about your business alone, cast a wider net by finding common ground with other businesses to form a group blog. When you start a blog with like-minded businesses, you can create a buzz that reaches a wide audience.

GROUP BLOGS

Let's examine how a group blog works. The blog "Word Wenches: Seven Authors, Plotting in the Present, Writing about the Past, and Improvising the Rest" (wordwenches.typepad.com) is a group blog. The blog's statistics are listed in a sidebar: years published—136; novels published—203; novellas published—71; range of story dates—9 centuries (1026–present).

Their blog posts are sometimes long (after all they are novelists), but they are chatty as they delve into historical information that their readers lap up. The Word Wenches also conduct lively discussions on their blog with other authors.

The Word Wenches are a good example of how a group blog can expand each member's target audience by linking similar interests while helping the customers. For more, visit www.wordwenches.typepad.com.

GUEST BLOGGING

Don't think you have to do it alone. You can invite others to post on your blog. Make it part of your blog's plan. For example, a tech company that specializes in networking solutions for businesses could structure its blog as follows:

Week 1: Tech tips

Week 1: Invite an ergonomic specialist to post on what readers need to know about their body mechanics if they sit and pound their keyboards day after day

Week 2: Tech tips

Week 2: Short post on storm surges and how to protect your equipment

Week 3: Invite an ophthalmologist to post about ways to reduce eyestrain

Week 3: Ask a tech

Week 4: Tech tips

Week 4: Talk about what kinds of fun things our readers can do this weekend

Another advantage in spreading out the workload is that you tap into all the resources your guest blogger can offer. The eye doctor who is scheduled to guest blog in week three doesn't have his own blog, but he has been telling his patients to be sure to read his post when it is published. This is a great way to get new customers. If you can be the catalyst that brings together like-minded people who service a similar audience, you will be seen as the leader of that online community.

By the way, the last item in the proposed blog schedule may surprise you; but you don't have to talk about business all the time. Spread it out. Think about *all* the things your customers do and are interested in. Believe it or not, these types of posts help your readers remember you next time they need tech services.

Step-by-Step Formula for the Perfect Blog

1. Determine who your audience is. What are you going to say to your readers that is going to be unique? Who will you talk to? Find a niche to find success because a blog or any business that aims to serve an audience that is too broad and nondefined is set to fail.

2. Get a catchy name that extends your business's branding. The right one makes the blog memorable.

3. Determine what interactive tools you will use on your blog. Will your blog use audio or video or both?

4. Find the right provider. Once you know what elements you want to use to enhance your blog, choosing the right provider becomes clear. If you are using video, you may need to invest in a blog that offers enough space to store it.

5. Create content that is of value to your customers. Offer tips, information, questions and answers, interviews, and insights not available in other places.

6. Start posting. Create several posts on your blog so that there's enough content when you send the word out. Commit to blogging at least two to three times per week.

7. Submit your blog to major blog banks.

8. Tell people about your blog. Send an e-mail to your customers and anyone you know who will be interested. Invite people to read your blog.

How to Say It with Your Blog

- Name your blog so it reflects what you'll be talking about as it relates directly to your business.

- Keep your blog on focus with themes.

- Find a provider that offers all the technical elements you need to create an effective blog.

- Keep the same look and feel as your other marketing products—both online and offline.

- Keep the tone casual. Be authentic, natural, honest, and informal, but maintain professionalism.

- Enhance your blog with other media such as photos, audio, and video.

- Say what you think about industry information; personalize your posts with your own views. Take a stand.

- Offer valuable information with news, trends, tips, insights, or analyses.

- Be brief. Blog posts are small, but frequent, snippets of information.

- Commit to consistency. Plan on blogging at least two to three times a week.

- Be a connector. Link to source information for background information on a topic.

- Expand your community with blogrolls.

- Inspire interactivity with reader comments and by posting on other blogs.

- Distribute your blog using RSS feeds for maximum exposure.

How *Not* to Say It with Your Blog

- Don't bombard your readers with listings and blatant advertising.

- Don't write in a stilted, awkward manner.

- Don't recite industry information without adding in your own thoughts.

- Don't write an essay.

- Don't be wishy-washy. Take a stand on the topic.

- Don't post without proofreading your text.

- Don't let a week go by without posting.

- Don't use vague subject headings such as "Hello world!" or "Vacation."

- Don't rely on just text—insert images, video, and audio. Spice up your blog.

Part Five

Getting Your Message Across … With a Podcast

NINE

PODCASTING ESSENTIALS

In today's world, rapidly changing technology continues to affect how information is consumed. Podcasting is quickly moving to the forefront of business communication. In January 2008, eMarketer, the leading analyst of online marketing trends, forecasted that while 6.5 million people would download a podcast once a week by the end of 2008, 25 million people would be regular podcast listeners by 2012.[10] Although podcasting requires more work than the other new media tools, it can be one of the most rewarding pursuits.

Podcasting is the youngest sibling of the new media suite. As the verbal and visual complement to e-zines and blogs, this tool is for anyone who likes show-and-tell. With both audio and video capabilities, podcasts offer you an opportunity to expand on your message in a way that aligns with your learning style and the style of your customers.

For the business owner, audio podcasts are for anyone who has the gift of gab. If you cringe at the thought of sitting down and writing articles or blog posts, this medium may be perfect for you. Whether it's you talking alone or you interviewing industry experts and talking to your best customers about their challenges, podcasts offer you the opportunity to discuss your business.

Instead of typing out your words for a reading audience (as for a website, e-zine, or blog), a podcast allows you to speak directly to your audience.

Video podcasts offer you the double advantage of talking about and showing your product to your audience. Consider a video if your business has plenty of stunning visuals that are specifically related to your business. A bed-and-breakfast owner could create a video podcast of a beautiful sunset shot from a guest-room's balcony or some peeks into local gardens that will be open to the public during August. Video podcasts are ideal for businesses in real estate, retail trade, accommodation, food services, and the arts as well as for businesses that can excite their audience with pictures and words together. Video podcasts are especially popular with travel and tourism offices because they are the ideal vehicle for showcasing a region's attractions.

Audio podcasts are pure sound and offer you a chance to talk about a wide variety of topics. Audio podcasts are perfect for interviews, quick tips, analyses, and advice. Consider using audio podcasts if you are in the professional, administrative, or information services because of limited visual content.

As with the entire set of new media products, podcasts work best when they are connected with your website, e-zine, and blog. Podcasts are web-based and can be distributed via RSS feeds. You'll need a podcast hosting service, and you'll want your podcasts to hyperlink with your website and blog.

Podcasting can be used by anyone who wants to get the word out about his or her business or organization and has an oral or visual message to convey. Think of podcasting if you've always wanted your own talk show, if you're a musician who wants to build up a fan base, if you're a speaker or seminar leader who wants new clients, or if you're an author who wants a wider readership. A school principal or superintendent might use a weekly podcast to touch base with her teachers, parents, and students.

Your new media products work together best when they offer variations on the same theme. For example, if you are a coffee purveyor, your theme for the month may be little-known coffees from Central America. In your e-zine, your main article could be about the benefits of Guatemalan coffee. Your blog would offer your customers a space to discuss their tasting preferences, and your video podcast could be sights and sounds from a coffee plantation in Guatemala along with your narration. You could also have an audio podcast of an interview with an exporter about the importance of choosing coffees that adhere to best practices. On your website, you could spotlight Guatemalan coffees and run a month-long special on those blends.

When all of your new media products are integrated, they enhance and complement each other. When potential customers find your podcast on a podcast directory they might like what they see so much that they subscribe to your e-zine and start reading your blog. By using all new media components, you offer different access points for interested new and existing customers.

The question of how often to podcast depends on how many new media tools you will use. For example, if you choose to use podcasts as a stand-alone marketing outreach tool, consider podcasting at least twice per week. But if you are using coordinated new media tools, as we strongly suggest, podcasting about twice per month will suffice.

Both audio and video podcasts can be delivered to your audience via an RSS feed. If a customer subscribes to your podcast, then his *podcatcher*, or podcast distribution tool, will deliver it directly to his computer when he starts the software. Podcatcher software allows your customers to listen or watch your podcast directly from their computer. Another important aspect is that your subscribers can add your podcast to their favorite mp3 player, so they can listen whenever and wherever it is convenient: at the gym, while walking the dog, or when commuting to work. This is a key reason for keeping your podcast under thirty minutes (or even shorter): You want your content to be just long enough to get your message across but short enough that clients can listen to the entire broadcast in a single bit of free time.

The trick to making your podcast compelling, as with all new media, is to offer quality content that attracts your customers' interest and offers value by solving a problem or giving them insight into a challenge.

Like your e-zine and blog, your podcast offers a chance to speak to your customer directly, extend your brand, and build your community. As podcasting technology grows, businesses that embrace this medium will be considered cutting edge. And all the new media marketing products you use will positively affect your bottom line.

Creating Symmetry among Your New Media Products

As noted earlier, you can use your podcast as a stand-alone product but you get more powerful results when you use it in combination with your blog, e-zine, and website. Because both blogs and podcasts use RSS feed technology to automatically deliver content to your audience, it makes sense to add a podcast feed icon to your blog. Be sure to promote your blog in your podcast by reminding your subscribers that they can go to your blog to make comments and join the discussion.

In each issue of your e-zine, be sure to include a box that describes your podcasts and lists the titles of the latest three episodes. Add the link to your website's podcasts page or to your blog so your readers can subscribe.

Your website is the hub of your new media marketing tools. All podcast hosting services offer a web page that can be linked to your site. Alternatively, archive or list your audio files on your website's podcast page so your clients can easily download the files.

Grab Podcast Listeners with a Compelling Name

You want your podcast to be an integrated part of your new media marketing, and your audience should readily recognize it as part of your brand. The title of your podcast could simply be the name of your business with the word *podcast* appended to the title. Better yet, you could give each new media tool a unique but related name. For example, your e-zine could be titled "Your Life, Your Business E-zine"; your blog, "Life and Biz Blog"; and your podcast "This Is Your Life, This Is Your Business Podcast."

If you decide not to give all your new media components the same title or related titles, decide on the type of content that you are going to share with your audience—and name your podcast accordingly. But it is best to stay with a name that links you, your business, and all your new media publications and broadcasts.

You want to use a title that will jump out and beckon potential customers to listen in. Your podcast name should speak directly to your audience's needs.

Because time is a precious commodity in today's busy world, give your subscribers information that can help them manage their tasks, quickly gain insight into some aspect of their business, or solve a life problem. Your podcast title should reflect the value you offer subscribers; the name should make a potential listener think, "Hey, that's what I've been looking for; this podcast can help me with my challenges and give me a better perspective."

The first step is to create an umbrella name that will say exactly what you're podcasting about. It should also pique your listeners' curiosity, align with their needs, or state a benefit. Choose a title that your audience will immediately identify with or that will intrigue them. Using the earlier example, "This Is Your Life! This Is Your Business!" makes it obvious to listeners that the podcast will help them find ways to integrate their business and personal lives.

The title of your podcast will lay the foundation for the content that will run throughout your broadcasts. Once you have the name for your podcast, all episodes should focus on the intended content in some way. For example, the episodes in the "This Is Your Life! This Is Your Business!" podcast could expand on the following monthly themes. Note that the title of each episode relates to both the theme and the overall podcast name.

Monthly Theme	Title of Podcast
Decluttering	Clear the Clutter, Clear Your Mind
Money management	Are You Taking Advantage of the New Tax Laws?
Feeling overwhelmed	Take Control Now!
Staying focused	*The 7 Habits of Highly Effective People*—Revisited
Wellness	Ten Ways to Recharge Your Inner Batteries

When your audience views the list of available podcasts on your website, the titles should trigger a strong and immediate response. Consequently, when you're developing a name for an episode, you must know your target audience. Know your potential and existing clients and what they need, then create informative podcasts that meet those needs.

With all the opportunities available to boost your marketing efforts, it is evident that creating a strategic name is a powerful aspect of marketing with your podcast.

What a Theme Can Do for Your Podcast

As with the rest of your new media tools, your podcast should not be a hodgepodge of episodes covering a variety of subjects without an overriding focus. Talking about the topic that you are covering in your e-zine and blog is a surefire way to ramp up your marketing efforts. If your audience didn't respond to you one way, they may respond in another way. Plus, speaking on that same theme covered by your e-zine and blog is a way to present a deeper and broader perspective on your theme. If your e-zine and blog are focusing on clutter control, find ways to use your podcast to inform and entertain your audience while staying on that topic.

When your audience has received and read your e-zine, interacted with you and others on your blog, and then heard you interview someone on the same subject, you will undoubtedly be perceived as the expert in this realm. In addition, your visibility and expert status is increased twofold when your audience can see and hear you in a video podcast.

Industry-Specific Tips: Podcast Content

Finance and insurance (financial consultant): Theme = teaching business owners how to use financial software; video podcast = how to use QuickBooks; audio podcast = five important software features and how to use them

Accommodations (jet service owner): In-flight video podcast = how to improve your golf swing; in-flight audio podcast = top best business books reviewed

Food services (caterer): Theme = wedding foods you can make at home; video podcast = how to make a popular appetizer; audio podcast = what's fresh at the farmers' market

Healthcare (medical facility): Theme = a year-long plan for better health; video podcast = demonstration of stretching exercises; audio podcast = musical accompaniment and tips for a twenty-minute walk

Retail trade (clothing in hard-to-find sizes): Theme = getting ready for prom; video podcast = dress styles for different body types; audio podcast = what's new in color and fabric

Technology Essentials

Of all the new media components, a podcast requires the most amount of technical skill; but don't be discouraged, it's not difficult to use. To *listen* to or *view* a podcast, your clients need a computer and a high-speed Internet connection, which most of your customers or clients already have. If your customers want to listen to your audio podcast when they're away from the computer, podcatching software will let them transfer it to their mp3 player. However, *creating* a podcast requires a number of tools.

Audio Podcasting

SOFTWARE

Beginner podcasters might want to try a free recording and sound-editing program before committing to full-featured, expensive software. Audacity (audacity.sourceforge.net) is a popular program and is available as a free download. However, once you get used to podcasting with a basic audio program, you will probably want to switch to more sophisticated software.

If you are going to create audio podcasts on a regular basis, consider buying a premium audio-editing system. Adobe Audition (www.adobe.com/products/audition) is one such program. This software is not inexpensive, but it will help you create good-quality productions. Audition's professional-level, multitask audio-editing capabilities allow you to record and edit clear, crisp audios. Adobe offers a free trial version, so you can give it a try before you commit.

Podcasters who don't want to worry about the technical aspects of recording can look to one-stop professional podcasting solutions. If you're looking for a free service, FreeConference (www.freeconferencecalls.com) offers a conference call service, which can record your content. Your audio can be sent to you as an mp3 file. If you want to create broadcast-quality podcasts and professional-looking videos, check out Audio Acrobat (www.audioacrobat .com), a comprehensive podcast service. Although the technical aspects of using a podcast service are minimal, be sure to examine the offered features. Some of these businesses do not provide editing, which means you'll have to run your podcast through another program to remove any extraneous sounds or redundant material or to cut the length of the podcast. Another option is to outsource the editing, once you have made the initial recording.

EQUIPMENT

Buy the best-quality microphone you can afford. A microphone that plugs into your computer's USB port generally produces better sound than one that plugs into your computer's microphone input. If you plan to conduct interviews or have guests on your podcasts, you may need a mixer for multiple inputs. Consult an audiovisual professional for detailed advice.

Also consider buying headphones so that you can listen to the quality of your podcast recording. Headphones allow you to focus exclusively on your sound quality and hear what your audience will hear.

Video Podcasting

SOFTWARE AND EQUIPMENT

Our society has grown accustomed to receiving information through videos, whether on television, DVDs, or online. Video can be one of the most powerful ways for you as a business owner to get your message across.

If you decide to produce videos, you will need a fairly good video camera. Digital equipment is constantly changing, so we suggest visiting a local electronic store. A knowledgeable sales assistant will be able to guide you to the camera that meets your specific needs.

You'll also need a good video-editing program. Most computers come with a basic program already installed on the hard drive. Many video cameras also come with basic editing software. These programs are good ways to gain some experience with editing video. If you decide that you will produce video podcasts on a regular basis, you will definitely want to purchase a more professional program. Apple's Final Cut Pro is an example of a high-end video-editing program for those who use a Macintosh computer. PC users may want to consider Pinnacle Studio Ultimate or Power Director as leading software choices under $100.

FILMING

When filming your podcast, be sure to capture more video than you think you will need, and don't forget to shoot from a variety of angles: close-up, medium, and long shots as well as straight on and from the side. Try to capture a steady image for at least ten seconds per shot, so you have options when you edit the video. You may want to consider taking a basic video production class at your local community college. You'll learn a variety of basic skills such as how to capture images in a sequence, lighting and sound techniques, how to work with graphics, and advanced editing techniques that can make your video podcasts spectacular.

How to Choose a Hosting Service

Once you've recorded your podcast you must send it to a remote server so that your subscribers can find it on the Internet. It's best to look for a host that offers a large amount of storage space. The size you need depends on how often you plan to podcast. Remember video podcasts need far more space than do audio podcasts. Your web hosting service may provide podcast hosting as part of your monthly fee or for a nominal additional fee. Or you may want to consider any of the following top podcast hosting services.

SWITCHPOD

Switchpod (www.switchpod.com) offers a variety of plans and is a good choice for the beginning podcaster. However, it also includes an expanded set of features for the more experienced podcaster. Offering free hosting to low-per-month packages, this is a good provider for a variety of business owners. This hosting service provides storage space for audio and video files. Subscribers can opt for free podcasts that feature ads; the paid service distributes ad-free podcasts. Swtichpod can also create automatic RSS feeds.

LIBERATED SYNDICATION

One of the most popular podcast hosting services is Liberated Syndication (www.libsyn.com), which offers several hosting plans with different monthly fees and storage space. Bandwidth is unlimited, so you will never pay overage charges. Liberated Syndication also provides a complete blog and podcast package that allows you to upload both audio and video podcasts and write an associated blog entry; an RSS feed is automatically created.

GODADDY

GoDaddy (www.godaddy.com), better known for domain hosting, offers podcast hosting services. There are several hosting plans, and price depends on the features provided. You can customize one of GoDaddy's templates to create a personalized look.

Core Essentials

Your podcast provides a platform from which you can speak your truth and offer your customers information that will make a difference in their lives. Committing to podcasting lets your audience know that they can depend on learning from you on a regular basis. Knowing what your customers want and need will help you create compelling content. And speaking your truth means that you sound like yourself and not what you think a polished broadcaster should sound like. It also means that you convey sincerity.

Put Your Heart into Your Podcast

Emerson wrote "Nothing great was ever achieved without enthusiasm." Infuse your talk with enthusiasm. Even though your audience can't see you when they listen to your audio podcast, they will be able to tell if you are passionate about what you are saying. Smile before you begin, it will translate into your voice. Remember to breathe naturally. Speak conversationally and naturally, as if you were talking face-to-face with a single customer. If you normally use your hands or use exaggerated facial gestures when you speak, don't be afraid to do so when making your audio podcast recording. Be sure to listen critically to your finished audio file: Does it sound like you being you? Speak to your audience with passion and sincerity. This medium can drive home your authenticity like no other.

Liven Up Your Talk

Create a picture with your words so your audience can "see" what you're talking about as they listen to your audio podcast. Use adjectives and other descriptive words to create vivid images. Think of how radio stories are enhanced when the speaker varies his or her tone. When filming a video podcast, your words should pertain to what is being seen. Don't show a beautiful sunset if your podcast is about ways to declutter a home office. Customers want to see what you are talking about.

Practice Your Enunciation

Speak clearly into the microphone and avoid mumbling; diction is important. If you are from a region that says *zinc* for "sink" or *sawr* for "saw" or *hunerd* for "hundred," you may want to practice saying those pesky words before they trip you up in your podcast. There are many more of these regional words or mispronunciations that you may *undoubtably* (undoubtedly) use, so streamline your vocabulary and rehearse your text before you record your podcast. If you want to brand your podcast as folksy, just make sure you have a folksy-type audience that will appreciate this kind of speech: *"Here's your sharpnin' the sawr podcast."*

Eliminate Filler Words

Some people think using *uhms* and *ers* make a podcast sound relaxed, natural, or even thoughtful. It doesn't. Fillers serve only to distract your audience from your message, and your listeners will switch your podcast off in a hurry.

Also limit the use of unnecessary connecting words, such as *well*, *and*, *like*, *y'know*, *yet*, *so*, and—the worst one—*okay*. The best way to avoid these pitfalls is to stay focused and to prepare what you want to say or have talking points. If you need to gather your thoughts, pause for a second. A moment of silence will allow you to catch your breath. And you can always edit out the silence later.

Creating Compelling Content

As mentioned throughout this book, when it comes to being successful with new media marketing, the operative word is always *value*. Without offering value, you will lose your customers. As a result, make sure that your podcast content is useful to your listeners. This is true no matter what type of business you own.

Almost everyone in your audience is feeling pressed for time; thus few want to commit to listening to a podcast longer than twenty or thirty minutes. Rather than recording a college-level lecture, offer your customers shorter bits of valuable and interesting information. If your podcast is under twenty minutes, you'll be more likely to capture subscribers who listen while on the run.

When you set up any of the new media components, it's important to evaluate the key benefits you offer to customers or clients. If you offer an intangible service, think about how you could provide meaningful audio or video material for your audience. For example, if you're a family therapist, you could create a video podcast showing how to use a family calendar to keep track of everyone's chores and appointments and discussing how this will eliminate arguments and stress.

If you are an exterminator, you might not want to create a video podcast of a cockroach infestation. Your clients don't want to see bugs—that's what they hire you for! You could, however, create an audio or video podcast focusing on giving one's home a good spring cleaning. After all, your service is the underlying foundation of a clean home, and your customers will appreciate your advice.

Be creative. Audio and video podcasts can effectively build a strong online presence.

Industry-Specific Tips: Compelling Podcasts

Insurance (national insurance network): Podcasts geared to affiliate agents to discuss the newest products and services

Government (police chief): Podcasts directed to the local community to discuss new laws

Social assistance (large foundation): Podcasts directed to grantees to discuss future projects

What Kind of Content Do You Want to Create?

Podcasting communicates using sounds and pictures, so don't forget to take advantage of these features. When creating audio podcasts, think beyond the words. What would your customers want to *listen* to rather than read about? What service or information is easier to talk about than to write about? When creating video podcasts, make sure the images are compelling and add to the content. What can you offer that is much better shown in pictures than described in words?

VIDEO OF YOUR BUSINESS'S KEY OFFERINGS

One good use of video podcasts is to show how your product or service can be used in an innovative way; the idea is not to blatantly push your product but to help your customers. Remember the needs of your audience and find ways to use video to meet those needs. For example, many furniture shoppers are drawn to makeover shows. For a video podcast, consider showing interesting customer makeovers featuring your furniture in their home.

People who frequent high-tech retail shops are interested in the latest gadgets. Video demonstrations of the hottest products found in your store would be a big draw. Take your camera to a trade show and film the vendors (after asking permission) using the cutting-edge models you'll be selling this year.

A person who stages homes (improving the look of a home to make it more appealing to buyers) could create a slide show of before and after pictures; the voiceover could point out the changes that were key to making the sale.

INTERVIEWS

Interviews make great audio podcasts. And while you may use interviews as fodder for other new media components, podcasting presents a more personal experience.

If you want to present your podcast in real time, it is important to organize your questions and comments. Be sure to conduct your interview in a quiet area. And be aware of your tone and voice inflection.

When interviewing someone for the other new media components (website, e-zine, and blog), you can e-mail questions, conduct a chat, and follow up days later to clarify a point or ask another question. Once you have finished your interview, you can sort through the information and write up your article or blog post. When you are recording an interview for use as an audio podcast, you don't have these luxuries.

Remember, however, that a single interview can be used across all of your new media tools. Your podcast could contain the entire interview or just a particularly compelling story. Your e-zine article could contain a few memorable quotes, whereas your blog post could discuss the interview experience in general. Use your website to show some photos and publish a transcript of the interview (if the entire interview was used for your podcast, use your website to publish two or three of the most interesting questions and answers). Each new media component should direct your audience to your other new media tools. Leveraging this one interview over multiple components is time efficient. You can create a number of different products from one ten-minute interview.

Who should you interview? Consider offering a compelling interview with an industry leader or someone who can offer insight into your specific field. The more valuable information the interviewee can provide the better. Try to ask the questions that many of your customers have wondered about. Don't be afraid to try to contact a well-known expert. Here are two ideas: (1) Carry an audio recorder to a trade show and ask a vendor or other expert if you can ask him or her a few questions. Or (2) visit PR Newswire (www.prnewswire.com) to find the latest information in your industry. Ask the person whose name is listed on the bottom of the release or the public relations representative or communications staff listed if you can interview the business leader mentioned in the release. It's best if you can do a brief telephone interview. Because interviews are primarily an exchange between two people, they work well as audio podcasts.

Interviewing Tips

When interviewing, remember to ask open-ended questions, not ones that can be answered with a simple yes or no. Remember to stay in the moment. Do not think of your next question while your guest is talking, pay attention to what he or she is saying; you don't want to miss a lead to a great follow-up question.

Invite people who have something new to say about your topic and from whom your audience wants to hear. Before the segment begins, be sure to do your homework. Nothing is worse than interviewers that don't know anything about their guest or the subject. When the interview begins, greet your guest warmly and put her at ease by starting off with subjects she wants to talk about.

Be tactful. While you want to allow your guest to finish her sentences, you don't allow her to ramble and lose focus. If you sense your guest is trailing off the topic, carefully rein her in by rephrasing the question.

Open-Ended Questions and Comments
How did you feel?
What did you say to that?

What effect did this have on _____?

Tell me a little about _____.

What is your role in _____?

Give the audience some insights into _____.

Describe _____.

What are the most important steps to _____?

How did you get started?

What happens next?

Where do you go from here?

What's the most surprising thing about your _____?

Who has inspired you along the way? How?

How have you changed since you _____?

PROFILES

Like interviews, profiles can do multiple duties for your new media components. They are similar to interviews because they may showcase a single individual. But you could also profile a business or industry. For example, your
podcast could contain a discussion with a community leader and a few sound
bites from people whose lives were positively affected by her work. Your blog
post could describe your own impressions of the leader, and your e-zine could
feature photos. You might use your website to publish a list of the good works
she has done for the community.

If your best customers are great examples of how your business can make
a difference, ask if you can profile them in an audio podcast. This works especially well if your client is well spoken. If you are a landscaper, a video podcast
is the way to go. Ask a client if you can film him enjoying his new butterfly
garden.

TIPS FROM YOUR BUSINESS

Consider creating a podcast that offers concrete advice in a logical, step-by-
step format. For example you could use a video podcast to show how to use a

particular feature in a popular software program you sell. Instead of recording a twenty-minute podcast of your top-ten tips, think about creating a series of short podcasts that cover only one tip each.

Industry-Specific Tips: Short Podcasts

Educational (tutoring service): Audio podcast presenting a word each day to help students build their vocabularies

Professional services (financial analyst): Audio podcast presenting a tip each week geared to a specific financial situation (retirement, college, taxes, vacation)

Healthcare (personal fitness trainer): Video podcast demonstrating an isometric exercise each month that can be done while sitting in front of the computer

A PANEL DISCUSSION

Almost every business interconnects in some areas with other businesses. Consider pooling your resources to create podcasts that would be worthwhile to not only your customers but those of your colleagues as well. For example, a patent attorney could ask a tax adviser and a manufacturing consultant to talk about important things customers need to know after they patent their product. This conversation could be used to collect material for e-zine articles and blog posts for all three experts.

A BEHIND-THE-SCENES LOOK

Traditional media ply viewers with behind-the-scenes footage of TV shows and movie sets, giving fans a chance to peek behind the curtain of success. Consider offering your own behind-the-scenes video podcast to introduce key staff and show off your offices. It humanizes your business and makes people realize you are more than just a name on the Internet. The best businesses that can use this to their advantage are manufacturing businesses, food services, the arts, and entertainment organizations.

Remember that you can also create podcasts that combine different elements. Perhaps you have a two-minute tip, a five-minute interview, and five-minute book review. Use all three segments, add some transitional material, and you have a well-rounded fifteen-minute podcast. To make things even easier, consider creating a basic template so your subscribers will know what to expect from your podcasts. But keep in mind that each component must offer value. It's better to have a shorter, more focused podcast than one with numerous segments that are weak overall.

Say It with Music

Because sound is such an important aspect of any podcast, consider including introductory music to set the mood and create a pleasant environment for your audience. Music can also be used as a bridge between segments of a podcast— like a pause before the next topic. You can choose from an eclectic variety of royalty-free music from several websites. Try Royalty Free Music Library (www.royaltyfreemusiclibrary.com) or do a web search for other vendors.

Consider your target audience when deciding on the kind of music to use. Are your subscribers mostly conservative bankers? If so, you may want to go easy on the new age sound. If you're targeting young people, check out what sounds are popular at the moment. Information services industries and upscale dining establishments might consider classical music, whereas more contemporary restaurants might want to use jazz. Healthcare and administrative industries could consider music that is upbeat and peppy. Therapists might want calm, soothing music. Think about the tone you are trying to convey through your business, and choose music to match it.

How to Say It: Interview Script

Once you have your theme, your equipment, your guest, and your music, you're ready to begin podcasting. For a sample script of a complete podcast, see "Protecting Your Investment" below. You don't necessarily have to write out a detailed script, but if it helps you organize your thoughts, use one. Make sure, though, that you don't sound like you're reading. You do not want to come off as rehearsed. On the other hand, even when you're not using a script, you should at least have some kind of guideline or outline.

Protecting Your Investment

Real estate agents have embraced podcasting as a potent tool to drive sales. Agent John Mason knows that his best customers are his existing ones. To stay top of mind, he created a podcast to help them get the most out of their purchase. Mason chose winterizing your home as the theme for the January edition of the Mountain Luxury Realty podcast.

PODCAST SCRIPT

FADE UP: Music (fifteen seconds)

FADE DOWN: Music fades out.

INTRODUCTION: Thanks for joining Mountain Luxury Realty's podcast. I'm John Mason. On today's show we have national expert Danny Linford, who will talk about how to winterize your home.

Well, if you're feeling a chill in the air, it's a good time to think about winterizing your home to reduce your heating bills; this is especially important if you live up in the mountains.

Danny Linford, host of his own popular Internet radio show, called "Today's Home Owner," has three quick money-saving tips to share with our listeners. Welcome, Danny. *[Mason has established his own and his guest's credibility. He sounds enthusiastic and welcoming.]*

DANNY: Thanks, John.

JOHN: So why should any homeowner even think about winterizing? *[Starts with an open-ended question.]*

DANNY: Look at how much money you spend on heating your home. The Department of Energy says it's about $1,400 per year. Winterizing could save you half of that.

There are three key steps you need to be aware of: First you have to inspect your insulation. The biggest place a house loses its heat is in the attic. If you can see your ceiling joists, you need more insulation. Second, you have to plug the gaps outside. And that means that caulk is your friend! You have to seal up all cracks on the outside of the home. That includes areas around windows and outdoor faucets, which can let in a tremendous amount of cold air. Then, in your third step, you're going to stop the leaks inside. Those cracks around windows, on perimeter walls, and around electrical outlets on exterior walls can create a tremendous leak of warm air.

JOHN: How much will all of that cost?

DANNY: A tube of caulk costs about $10. The window insulation kit costs $15, and each kit can cover three to five windows. But look how much you save. The estimated yearly saving is $60 to $80.

JOHN: Wow, those are great tips. Thanks, Danny, for stopping by. Now if someone wants to get ahold of you, how would he or she learn more?

DANNY: They can visit my website at www.dannylinford.com.

[To end the podcast, Mason compliments his guest and asks him to repeat his name and the URL for his website to make sure listeners remember them. Then Mason adds a two-sentence farewell, repeats his own name, and supplies his own website's URL.]

TEN

TELLING YOUR AUDIENCE ABOUT YOUR PODCASTS

Podcast-Distribution Tools

Podcasts, like blogs, require specific distribution tools to notify subscribers when a new episode is available. Your podcast hosting service, like GoDaddy (www.godaddy.com) or BlueHost (www.bluehost.com), will provide the basic tools needed to deliver your podcast to your listeners. Podcasts use the same feed delivery mechanisms as do blogs. See "Make Use of Blog-Distribution Tools" on page 132 for more information.

Gain Exposure with Your Podcast

Similar to blogs and e-zines, podcasts have their own directories. They run the gamut of general to specific. The rule when submitting any new media product to a directory is that more is more. Start with the largest directory and work your way down the list. Try to submit your podcast to as many directories as possible. You never know where your audience is. Set out a wide net by using the most popular directories, and then go deep and narrow by using niche directories. All the directories are free, so don't limit yourself.

Podcast Directories

iTunes, Podcast Alley, and Yahoo! Podcasts are some of the popular free directories to which you can submit your podcasts. These sites require registration and prompt you to classify your podcasts under different categories, so you can make sure it's easy for your target audience to find you.

With more than a hundred thousand podcasts in its directory—from big-name companies to independent creators—iTunes is an ideal place for your podcast. Because it is one of the leading sources for digital media on the web, many potential clients are likely to look there for informative podcasts. Customers who use an iPod can set iTunes to automatically download your podcast to the player whenever the devices are linked. It's quick and easy to add your podcast to iTunes. See the website (www.itunes.com) for more details.

Podcast Alley is a popular directory that also offers forums and links to resources for podcasters. One fun feature is their podcast top-ten list, created from votes from their listeners.

Yahoo! Podcasts is powered by the digital media giant Yahoo!, so there are numerous podcast listings with a huge audience. Another benefit is that it allows you and your listeners to tag your podcast in the description field so it can become even more searchable.

While podcast directories list almost any content that can be placed within a broad category, there are specialized podcast directories that service niches. Some podcast directories deal with books or book marketing; others deal exclusively with health issues. If your business or industry does not have its own specific podcast directory, focus on the larger directories. But if you can find an appropriate niche directory, be sure to register—this is a place your target audience turns to for information.

Industry-Specific Tips: Niched Podcast Directories

Education: American Writers Podcast (american_writers_podcast.vital podcasts.com)

Healthcare: Personal Growth Podcast Directory (www.personalgrowth podcastdirectory.com)

Administrative and support: Virtual Assistant Podcast Directory (www .virtualassistantpodcastdirectory.com)

Women-based business: Women in Business Podcast Directory (www .womeninbusinesspodcastdirectory.com)

Professional: Small Business Podcast Directory (www.smallbusinesspod castdirectory.com)

Technology: Technology Podcast Directory (www.technologypodcast directory.com)

Podcasting is a leading-edge marketing method to communicate with your audience. If you embrace this technology now you can be one of the first businesses on your block to get the word out using this medium, which provides you a competitive edge in all the business you do.

How to Say It with Your Podcasts

- Think about what value you can offer your clients with content that is visual and sounds appealing.

- Find a name that's compelling.

- Use a theme to help you create symmetry among all your new media products.

- Find content that is relevant, such as an interview or a book review.

- Sound sincere. You don't have to be a broadcaster to record your voice. Just be professional and enthusiastic. Remember that tone has a lot to do with how your message is received.

- When interviewing someone, ask open-ended questions. You don't have to be a professional journalist. Just be curious and ask who, what, where, when, why, and how to elicit interesting answers.

- Say it with a song. Adding royalty-free music at the beginning and end of your podcasts adds texture and interest. It also sets the tone. Remember you have to appeal to your audience's tastes.

- Talk with a joint venture partner on a topic that will serve both of your audiences.

- Create an audio podcast to go with your e-zine interview or blog profile.

- Add your podcast to a number of directories, both general and niche.

- Listen to other podcasts. Become part of the podcasting world by listening to a variety of other podcasts.

How *Not* to Say It with Your Podcasts

- Don't garble your words.

- Don't speak in a monotone.

- Don't record in a noisy environment.

- Don't bombard your readers with too much information.

- Don't use blaring, harsh music.

- Don't take on the persona of a newscaster or anyone else, just be yourself and use good grammar and voice modulation.

- Don't publish any podcast that is not relevant to your audience.

- Keep your podcasts short. Each segment should be no longer than five to ten minutes long.

- If you use multiple segments, use music to make the transitions.

Part Six

Putting It All Together

ELEVEN

GETTING THE WORD OUT ABOUT YOUR BUSINESS

Now that you have developed your website, e-zine, blog, and podcasts, you are ready to launch them into the world. It's not enough to create these powerful marketing tools and expect people to find them. In this section you'll learn how to promote your business with several proven marketing tactics such as the following:

Search engines. This is the first tool people use when they need to find something online. Making sure your business is at the top of the results list is critical if you want prospects to find your business. After clicking on the link to your website, they should find out who you are, discover the nature of your business, and make a decision about whether they want to become your client or customer.

Viral marketing. This is an important aspect of the interconnectivity of the Internet. The links to your new media products become your fingerprints in cyberspace. Post an article or report online, embed the URL to your website or blog, and the world can follow you to wherever you lead it.

Social media. These sites have become a transformative element in society. Like a magnet, they attract hundreds of millions of people around the world, offering a place where people meet and connect through a network of friends. The possibilities for spreading the word about your business to this global community are limitless.

Other tactics. The Internet allows you to attract attention to your business in numerous ways. Vast opportunities exist for you to join forces with like-minded businesses to create synergy and boost your business.

Search Engines

In the past, you'd spend hours in a library, thumbing through file cards or fanning through the yellow pages to locate information. Today, you type your search criteria into a search engine, and the information you seek appears in a matter of seconds.

In technical speak, spiders crawl blogs, social media, and networking sites more frequently than websites so if you post often on your blog (at least twice per week), your site will earn a high ranking.

According to HitWise, an online intelligence service, Google continues to rank highest in search engines, accounting for 66.4 percent of all searches in the United States in February 2008.[11] Yahoo! and MSN follow with Ask.com increasing its rank from the previous year.

When you list your website or blog at Google, Yahoo!, or any other search engine, you are asked to submit your website's name and URL, a brief description (these ten to twenty words show up under your link), and keywords (words associated with your content). You can also take a one-step approach and use a submission tool, such as Add Me! (www.addme.com), to submit your site to the most popular search engines.

Keywords

Because most potential website visitors will find your business through one of the major search engines, it's imperative to tag your website and blog with the right keywords—the words your prospects are likely to use when searching for a business like yours. Use your company name, including common typos, and each product and service you offer as keywords. Don't forget to use phrases, too, as web surfers may type in two or more words for their search.

Look at the material on your website, in your blog, in your e-zines articles, and in titles of your podcasts. Pick words you use frequently and that represent the content you offer. Finally, think about what words your customers would use if they were searching for your website.

Industry-Specific Tips: Keywords

Note: For each industry, the owner would also list his or her name, the name of the website, and the name of the business or shop.

Writer (business plan writing): Writing, business plan, writing business plans, marketing for small businesses, small business success, writing a business plan, writer for hire, business writer, financial writer, marketing writer, plan writer, business guru, writer genius, writers for business

Plumber (in Phoenix): Plumber, phoenix, plumber, area code 602, clogged drain, Arizona

Food services (doughnut shop): Doughnuts, cruller, latte, muffins, Boston cream, breakfast, coffee

Social assistance (daycare for autistic children in Denver): Autism, special-needs children, Denver daycare, autistic preschool

To get deeper insight into how Web surfers search for information, use an online search statistics tool, such as Yooter (www.yooter.com/keyword/overture.php). For each word you type into the search box, Yooter generates a list of the most commonly searched keywords and phrases, based on statistics from Yahoo! and MSN.

For example if you type the word *stroller* into Yooter's search box, you will discover that the most popular result is *"Maclaren stroller."* Next in the list of results are *stroller*, *baby stroller*, and *double stroller*. If you sell strollers, you just learned several marketing tips. First, you now know what keywords should be on your site. Second, you have gotten ideas about what to write in your e-zine and blog, what to talk about in your podcasts, and what to feature on your website. You have also learned that you need to stock, sell, and advertise Maclaren strollers.

Viral Marketing

The World Wide Web consists of a vast network of individual sites that are linked to each other in numerous ways. Savvy business owners have taken advantage of this interconnectivity by employing viral marketing.

Fear not, you won't need a vaccine. However, viral marketing can spread your message around the world as quickly as the flu can spread through a college dormitory. Viral marketing works like word of mouth, but because this is an online phenomenon, it has earned the nickname "word of mouse."

Viral marketing is one of the best ways to promote your new media products (website, e-zine, blog, and podcast). The objective is to create brand awareness and to inspire people to act on your one simple message. Your message could be for people to call you, sign up for a workshop, go to your site, or e-mail you. Viral marketing spreads the word about your business to millions of people around the world.

When it comes to sharing content, the operative words are *free* and *easy*.

The core idea of viral marketing is to produce linkable content that can be forwarded—such as articles, worksheets, audios, videos, slideshows, and software. Your content must always have your name and contact information at the end. This is a vital aspect of viral marketing.

When you produce your content, you want to elicit or trigger an emotional reaction. The goal is for readers to respond to and forward your content. It's the forwarding that puts the viral aspect in motion. Those people then forward it to even more people and so on. Before you're even aware of it, vast amounts of people have accessed and viewed your information then subscribed to your offerings.

Articles

Articles are the most popular and linkable means by which you can offer needed information to your readers. Articles are easily forwarded to others. See Parts Two and Three for more on articles.

Templates

A template can help your customers accomplish a challenging task. By providing your audience with the skills or tools to accomplish a particular job, you'll come to mind when they need additional help. Such an information tool positions you as the go-to person, the expert, for services. For example, a public relations specialist could create a press release template for her prospects and customers who want to garner media attention. The PR specialist could create a fill-in-the-blank form so all her customers have to do is add their own information where indicated.

A worksheet is a free information product that your customers can download from your website (with links appearing in your blog and e-zine and mentioned in your podcast) when they opt-in with an e-mail address. When potential and existing clients who use your worksheet realize immediate results, they will turn to you for more help. For example, the owner of an art gallery filled out the press release template mentioned earlier. He then got a call from the local newspaper, which wanted to profile his establishment. Two important consequences are that the potential client told his friends where he got the template (generating visitors to the PR specialist's website) and the gallery owner was contacted by a number of other media outlets. He then realized that he needed a PR manager, so he turned to the person whose template he used.

Audio and Video Products

Audios and videos can be interesting, entertaining, and informative viral tools. These productions can relate directly to your business or talk about the pain or challenges your target audience grapples with. According to a November 2006 study conducted by MarketingExperiments.com, a group of twenty-eight videos they created and distributed around the Internet yielded more than 320,000 views in a sixty-day period.[12] They concluded the same number of views using traditional pay-per-click advertising would have cost them at least $1,200. The videos were all shorter than five minutes and featured a website to visit at the conclusion.

Large companies have already realized the power of viral videos. For example, as part of Dove's Campaign for Real Beauty, the company has produced a series of short online videos to demonstrate the way beauty is perceived in our society. The marketing message is briefly displayed at the end of the video. At least one of the videos has been posted on YouTube (www.youtube.com); as of this writing it has been viewed nearly five million times. Dove's viral marketing strategy was so popular, that parodies of the original video popped up on the Internet; those videos created lots of buzz and increased the brand's exposure.

Industry-Specific Tips: Audio and video
Professional (law practice): Audio podcast of the top-ten best lawyer jokes that ends with a short promotion and permission to forward the episode

Retail trade (car manufacturer): Video podcast featuring new sleek designs that ends with the company logo and contact information

Food service (microbrewery owner): Video podcast showing how beer is made that ends with an announcement of the brewery's weekly beer-tasting event

Videos, especially, appeal to a wide audience. They can be part of a successful viral marketing campaign because a good video is likely to be posted on a public video website. For more about YouTube, see page 191.

Slideshows

With the help of basic software (such as PowerPoint), almost anyone can create a simple or elaborate slideshow that is motivational, inspiring, or informative. One idea is to create a step-by-step guide for completing a project. You can use free photos from an image bank on the web (for example, stock.XCHNG at www.sxc.hu) and many slide programs offer free design templates.

A slideshow could also consist of your own photographs; you could add audio (royalty-free music or a voiceover) to enhance your product. Think about ending your slideshow with an image of your logo, the name of your business, and the URL to your website. Post your slideshow on your website and be sure to add a link on your blog and in your e-zine so the video and link can be passed on to others.

Industry-Specific Tips: Slideshows

Religious (a minister): Interactive, customized slideshow that provides a daily inspirational message to parishioners that ends with an invitation to attend Sunday services

Educational services (learning center): Slideshow listing the ten steps to effective study habits for teens that ends with an offer for SAT tutoring

Political (candidate for mayor): Slideshow revealing the candidate's vision for community development that ends with a reminder to get out and vote

Software

If you are technologically savvy, you can write a bit of useful software (a plug-in, for example), create a game, or produce an interactive video. The best viral marketing tools are useful programs and fun games. If you don't know how to do computer programming, you can hire someone to create what you need. It may cost less than you think. Do an Internet search for a programmer or coder; one place to look is RentACoder (www.rentacoder.com).

When considering the creation of a program for distribution think about your monthly themes (see Parts Two through Four): What is currently relevant? Or look to pop culture; you can tie your business in to a spoof on a popular movie. Write a universally useful computer program, such as a budget tracker or a food diary.

In November 2007, OfficeMax created a fun program called Go Elf Yourself. Visitors to the website could upload up to four photos of themselves, family members, or friends, which were then superimposed on elves that danced to holiday music. The effect was so entertaining and delightful that the program was quickly shared with others on the Internet. The link on the bottom said "Click here to Elf Yourself." At the end of the e-mail was the following message: "This software brought to you by OfficeMax." Many potential customers may not have been thinking of OfficeMax during the holiday season, but this quirky program increased brand awareness as it circulated around the world and the company was even spotlighted on morning talk shows. According to OfficeMax, their Elf Yourself marketing campaign attracted more than 120 million visitors in December 2007.[13] It quickly became the best viral campaign in the history of the web.

Industry-Specific Tips: Promotional Software

Healthcare (dentist): A video of chattering teeth making wisecracks that ends with a reminder to see a dentist

Finance (tax accountant): Software that keeps track of business deductions

Food service (caterer): Party-planner program

E-mail Informal or Grassroots Letter

The simplicity of e-mail makes it an accessible way to get the word out about your business. You could send a grassroots letter to everyone you know—friends, relatives, neighbors, coworkers, business colleagues, customers, and prospects—informing them about the services you offer. Here's an example of what you could say in a grassroots letter to garner e-zine subscriptions:

Dear Jane,

Did you know that by using e-mail, e-zines, blogs, and podcasts you can spread the word about your business without spending a whole lot of money?

Our new e-zine, "Marketing with New Media," teaches you how to use websites, e-zines, blogs, and podcasts together to help you build a loyal community of customers. It also teaches you how to communicate with your audience using new media. Best of all, our tips help you do it all in less time at a lower cost than with traditional marketing methods.

Visit www.newmediamavens.com and subscribe today!

Feel free to give us a call at 704-780-1968 or send us an e-mail at mavens@ newmediamavens.com. Also please click on this "tell-a-friend" link to forward to others who you think may be interested in this information.

Sincerely,

Lena and Alison

The New Media Mavens

A grassroots letter can be a viral marketing tool that gets the word out about your business. Embed a link to a sample issue of your e-zine so you pass along valuable information.

Create an E-mail Signature

The free e-mail provider Hotmail was one of the first companies to take advantage of using an e-mail signature as a viral marketing tool. The company wanted to get the word out about their service, so they appended one line—"Get your private, free e-mail at www.hotmail.com"—as a footer in every e-mail. Hotmail's strategy worked because their marketing message was simple. Soon word spread like wildfire and their service quickly became one of the most popular e-mail services on the Internet.

Whenever you send e-mail, you can garner attention from your clients, customers, and prospects by adding an intriguing offer to your e-mail signature line. Your signature line should always include your basic data—your name, title, business, e-mail address, and telephone. Consider another line or two to announce updates of your website, e-zine, blog, or podcast. If your update or offer is compelling, your audience will follow the link to get more information. Many business owners leave their signature line static, but after a while people stop reading it. By updating your signature line, you offer one last chance to get your audience's attention in a subtle manner.

Your e-mail signature line is a viral marketing tool because it remains at the end of your message when your information e-mail is forwarded to others. The idea is to include an article or other free download that will drive readers to your website.

Industry-Specific Tips: E-mail Signatures
Food services (restaurant owner): Link to a video of the chef making the restaurant's signature dish; link to a blog post providing step-by-step instructions on how to carve a turkey

Wholesale trade (flooring company): Link to that week's sale item; link to a video teaching sales reps about a new product

Retail trade (vitamin store): Link to an e-zine article about plant statins; link to blog post about calcium

Planning a strategy to implement some or all of the tactics discussed in this chapter will jump-start your viral marketing campaign. A viral marketing campaign is a process that starts with creating your viral marketing message, whether it's directing people to do something or it's branding your company. Plan ways to deliver your message. The next step is to generate buzz with your content and attract prospects to your website. Encourage your web visitors to subscribe to your e-zine, download your free information product, and give you their e-mail address. Once you have their information, you can consistently entice them to become part of your community by using your e-zine, blog, and/or podcasts. Ultimately they may purchase your product or service.

A viral marketing campaign should not be an arbitrary solution or a quick fix but a vital part of your overall marketing plan. A solid viral marketing plan will result in solid results.

Social Media

Although viral marketing gets the word out about your business, social media brings the world in. According to a 2008 report by comScore, a leading Internet research company, the number of worldwide visitors to social networking sites has grown to 530 million, representing approximately two out of every three Internet users.[14] Social media leaders MySpace and Facebook are neck and neck and the study indicates that each one of the giants has more than 100 million visitors per month. As a force to be reckoned with, MySpace (www .myspace.com), Facebook (www.facebook.com), and YouTube (www.youtube

.com), among others, have drastically changed the way people connect with each other.

Social media sites allow you to set up a profile page, talk about who you are and what you do, and create your own visible network that others can tap into. The main benefit of the network is that it creates a community.

New social media sites pop up almost every day and their prowess shows no signs of slowing down. According to a 2006 research report from PQ Media, advertising on user-generated online media will grow to $757 million by 2010.[15] This represents emergent trends in communicating and requires a different mind-set from the traditional ways.

For businesses, the goal of venturing into social media should not be to hit people over the head with the message to buy your widget. Your goal is to attract community members who might sample your wares. Consequently, getting the word out about your business on a social media site is far different from traditional advertising. If there has ever been a place where organic small business marketing is most effective, it is on a social media site. Instead of pushing a product or blatantly self-promoting, businesses are encouraged to communicate honestly. Their newfound friends will give them direct feedback. It's for this reason that businesses who want to use social media sites must get clear on what their message is, who they want to attract to their profile page, and how they will open the lines of communication.

Social media sites offer an array of ways to connect with your audience with streaming audio and video, the ability to post pictures, and more. While social media sites offer you numerous ways to showcase what you have to offer, they are best when they enhance, not take the place of, your new media tools—your website, e-zine, blog, or podcasts. Rather, feature links on your social media site to gain attention for your new media tools and to build your audience.

First embraced by Hollywood as a key way to market movies to teenagers, the use of social media sites to promote a business has now become mainstream. According to a 2006 Pew Internet and American Life Project study, people not only socialize online but also incorporate the Internet into their quest for information and advice as they seek help and make decisions.[16] Before you plunge into the social media pool, or if you're already wading in the shallow end, it's best to make sure the waters you're swimming in are the same ones you will find your target audience in.

MySpace

With nearly two hundred million subscribers, MySpace has the largest membership of any of the social media sites. The site caters specifically to young people between the ages of sixteen and twenty-five and understands that their core audience wants to be cool and hip. It's a great site for businesses that cater to the teen and young adult demographic, such as artists, computer gaming companies, and musicians.

But MySpace is not only for kids. According to a 2006 report by the New Media Institute (NMI), the demographic composition of MySpace.com has changed considerably.[17] In previous years, half of the site's visitors were at least twenty-five years old, while today more than two-thirds of MySpace visitors are twenty-five or older. It has become even more likely that members of your target audience are on MySpace.

Take a look at the "groups" category on the site and see where your business could fit in. For example, the business and entrepreneurs category has more than twenty-four thousand different groups ranging from accounting to zombie aficionados.

Facebook

While MySpace is perceived as the social networking for teenagers, Facebook was designed originally for college students to network. It has branched out to become more inclusive and is increasingly popular with businesspeople and has a membership base of over seventy million. Facebook's largest audience is age thirty-five and older.

Singin' the Blues

Blues musician, singer/songwriter, and harmonica player Scott Albert Johnson has used his MySpace page (www.myspace.com/scottalbertjohnson) to promote his album *Umbrella Man* and has more than thirty thousand friends. With nearly ninety thousand views, his page features his concert dates, magazine articles, links to his band's website, musicians who have inspired him, and photos. The site also features streaming audio so when you first click on it you can hear the sounds of the harmonica on some of his amazing songs.

Johnson talks about his successes with MySpace.

What have been the benefits for you using MySpace?
I've been able to expose and, to some extent, sell my music to literally the entire world. It's been truly gratifying to get feedback (almost all of it positive) from so many people.

Have there been drawbacks?
There was one system crash that was a little scary, and it happened just as I was getting some exposure in a national music magazine. First my entire page crashed, and then it came back with only about 10 percent of my friend count. Fortunately, I was able to locate (through some serious sleuthing) two very cool and helpful MySpace techs who were able to fix the problem. But it made me realize how dependent I have become on MySpace for marketing my music.

What has been the biggest surprise?
I would say it's been the way that word spreads so quickly among like-minded people who are into the same types of music (or other interests). The more you work at marketing yourself this way, the more it starts to build its own momentum.

How did you get more than thirty thousand friends?
It was a combination of proactive outreach and positive word of mouth.

What strategies or advice would you like to share for other artists/entrepreneurs?
MySpace is one of several social networking tools that the independent artist has at his or her disposal. Don't be afraid to utilize it in every way possible.

The core focus of Facebook is groups, organized, for example, by region, school, or company. The key to mastering this site is to be involved with as many groups as possible and to present yourself to others. It's a very subtle medium in which you can post news and events, join discussions, or rally for a cause. The site's altruistic tone is a great place for social organizations, educational institutions, and even political candidates to host their site.

YouTube

According to a 2008 comScore research finding, online video has become the dominant online entertainment format, led by the global popularity of YouTube with more than 250 million visitors.[18] As the first and foremost free place on the Internet to share video content, YouTube can help businesses get massive exposure and is used by people aged eighteen to fifty-five. Due to its inherent sharing capability, it is considered a viral tool. You can embed the link in a blog post or on your website or forward it in an e-mail. The goal is to create an entertaining or informative video that will encourage comments.

The social interaction comes in when viewers comment on the video clip. Businesses who have created the most buzz using YouTube are the ones that have created the most over-the-top videos.

Blending for Entertainment

How do you make blenders sexy? The makers of Blendtec answered that question by making a series of hugely popular videos of their blenders chopping up anything and everything one could imagine. iPod? No problem. Marbles? You betcha! The company had such huge success with their videos, they now offer a DVD called *Will It Blend—The First 50 Videos* (www.willitblend.com) containing their videos and behind-the-scenes footage. The videos helped the sales of their home and commercial blenders skyrocket.

What to Say on Your Social Media Profile

No matter what site you use, the key is to communicate authentically about who you are and what you and your business are all about. These profiles take a nod from the informal tone of blogs and encourage personality. Create your page in your own name, not your business's. Talk about your business as one of your main interests, and remember to write about why you love it and what inspired you to start it in the first place. This is the place for your backstory, such as how you were spurred on to entrepreneurial pursuits after your first success with a lemonade stand at age five.

Talk about your product or service and how and why you developed it. If you liked studying bugs as a teen and now create products that help stimulate a love of science in young children, discuss why the science kit you sell is exactly the one you wish you'd had when you were a young person. Then post a picture of the kit and link to the product's point of purchase.

Ask your social media friends for their input about what you offer. But remember you're part of a give-and-take community. Commit to being part of it by offering your feedback on your social media friends' pages, too.

Industry-Specific Tips: Social Media Profiles

Educational services (acting coach): Profile discusses why he became an actor, lists links to movies he has worked on, lists actors who influenced him, and talks about the coaching services he offers

Professional (orchid breeder and nursery owner): Profile talks about her love of plants, why she is passionate about orchids, photos of her favorite cultivars, coupons for her store, and links to her new media publications

Food services (pastry chef): Profile includes photos of newlyweds with their wedding cake, stories about helping his grandfather at his bakery in Austria, recipes, and a link to his website

Attracting Friends

Each social media site offers a way to attract friends, or other members of the site, to your community. It's an interesting fact of the Internet: People who would not feel comfortable saying hello to strangers on the street are perfectly okay with inviting those same people to become part of their online community. As a business owner, your goal is to reach out to as many people as you feel would be interested in your community.

To invite friends, go to the site's search area and select the characteristics of your target audience. You can select religious background, age, geographical location, sexual orientation, body type, education, income, and more.

Once you find the group of people who fit the characteristics you searched for, you can automatically invite them to become your friend with the click of a mouse. This is somewhat of a scattershot approach. A better bet is to add a personal message to your invitation or to send these people a message asking them to visit your page and read your profile. In your invitation, tell your potential friends why you are inviting them and what you think would interest them in your profile.

For example, let's say you want to expand your bookstore's reading group and you have a target audience of single and divorced women between the ages of thirty-five and fifty-five who live within a twenty-mile radius of your store. Conduct a search and invite the women whose names pop up to become your bookstore's friend by sending them this hypothetical introductory note:

> Hi! I'm Jan Hook, owner of Hook's Books. I'd like to invite you to check out my profile. Every week, I review the best in women's fiction and offer discounts on the top three books, as voted on by my friends. You are also invited to come to my bookstore for a party we hold each month for new members of our reading clubs. We meet once a month with other women in the Seattle area. You can see our full book club schedule on my profile. I look forward to meeting you soon!

Industry-Specific Tips: Attracting Friends

Educational (tennis instructor): Target audience = individuals over the age of thirty-five who earn more than $50,000 a year; profile page incentive = videos of tennis clinics

Healthcare (yoga studio owner): Target audience = local parents of young children; profile page incentive = coupon for yoga classes for children

Manufacturing (maker of fine leather gloves): Target audience = women over forty years old who make more than $100,000 a year; profile page incentive = guide to caring for leather

Business owners may wonder what impact they will see on their bottom line as a result of meeting a group of people online. First, the sheer number of people you'll have the opportunity to interact with online is more than you would meet in the normal course of offline business. Remember, it's a numbers game. Hundreds of millions of people are members of social media sites, so if even a small percentage of them are impressed with what you offer, you have still reached a lot of people. All of those people are potential customers.

Second, you cannot afford to bypass these networks. Social media sites have transformed how and where people communicate online; you and your business need to be part of it.

Social Media Sites Expand Their Horizons

Every day social media sites pop up with a new focus on specific target audiences. Ivory Madison launched Red Room (www.redroom.com), a social media site for the literary world, at the beginning of 2008. It is already home to hundreds of authors, including numerous bestsellers, such as Barack Obama (Democratic presidential candidate and author of *Dreams of My Father* and *The Audacity of Hope*), Amy Tan (author of *The Joy Luck Club* and others), and Khaled Hosseini (author of *The Kite Runner* and *A Thousand Splendid Suns*).

"Redroom.com is a place for writers and readers," said Madison, Red Room's founder and chief executive officer. "In the Web 2.0 community the philosophy is that a website doesn't reach its maximum impact until you have members help to create value. The real value is in the thousands of voices you wouldn't have heard otherwise. Technology makes it easy and affordable for readers to do this."

The idea for the site was a natural extension for Madison, who had created a highly successful real-life salon for writers in San Francisco, California, called the Red Room Writers Society. "What we did was help writers finish the books they were working on, making their dreams come true," she said. "The website was born out of the desire to provide a place where writers could showcase their work and help those who might be intimidated by technology. Our goal is to help writers with the business side while also building a great community."

Professional Networking

LinkedIn (www.linkedin.com) and Ryze (www.ryze.com) focus on people connecting and networking with a large professional audience. These sites supercharge professional networking in the traditional sense. They take the old-fashioned idea of introductions and exchanging business cards to a virtual level. Here's how it works: You register and list your jobs, education, skills, and accomplishments. Then you send an e-mail inviting your colleagues and friends to join your network. Once your colleagues register and add their contacts, you can browse the network you have started and ask to be introduced to others in the group.

Small business owners have used these tools to help them find potential clients, market their businesses, and make valuable connections. LinkedIn has risen to become the most popular. One of the most important benefits of being a LinkedIn member is that it raises your individual search engine profile. When someone searches for your name, your LinkedIn profile often appears either as a first listing or on the first page of the search results.

Getting the Word Out Some More

Although search engines, viral marketing, and social media sites are ideal ways to help you attract your audience, other methods exist. Integrate your offline tactics into your online marketing efforts to create a seamless blend. You can also get the word out about your business by speaking to your audience and writing press releases to a variety of news media.

Speaking

Speaking is an offline marketing tactic that can attract tons of visitors to your site. Simply point your audience to your online viral marketing product (such as your free e-book download) during or after each talk. Collect your audience's e-mail addresses so that they can become part of your online community. At the end of your talk, be sure to mention that the dates and topics of all your upcoming speaking engagements are available on your website.

Online Strategic Alliances

The members of your target audience will generally be interested in related businesses and products. If you sell athletic clothing for elite runners, then your customer base is also interested in running shoes, sports drinks and bars, and even gym bags.

Make friends with the owners of complementary businesses. This is where creating a strategic partnership comes in. Think of providing reciprocal or referral links on each other's website; write a note to the business owner suggesting this and send a copy to his or her webmaster. Once you've shared links, open a discussion about posting to each other's blog and interviewing each other for your e-zines.

Sponsors

If you can create great video that becomes a big hit on a video-sharing site, you'll attract hordes of traffic to your website or blog. This traffic will give you leverage when you solicit sponsors to advertise on your site. If at the end of your video, the URL provided takes viewers to a web page listing your seminars and workshops, that's the page on which you'll place your sponsors' ads. Solicit companies that share your target audience, provide them with your website statistics, and offer them the opportunity to place their ad on your site. Charge them an agreed-on fee. The audience that you attract must be a likely audience for your sponsors, making it a win-win situation.

The big difference between sponsorships and strategic alliances/partnerships is that sponsors pay to be on your new media component; a strategic partnership offers free, reciprocal endorsements.

Listservs, Groups, and Forums

Almost from its start, the Internet has made networking and building community easy. There are e-mail lists (also called mailing lists or Listservs) and groups for every interest, and the numbers keep growing. A group in this sense is a discussion list that takes place through e-mail. Here's how to establish your business with the right group:

1. Identify a group on the Internet that aligns with your interest or your business. For example, visit a group hosting site like Yahoo! Groups (www .groups.yahoo.com) or Google Groups (www.groups.google.com) or an industry-specific host such as AuthorNation (www.authornation.com).

2. Register with the group. Watch the posts for a while to get the gist of the conversations and learn how you can help. For example, if you are a lawyer whose target audience is small businesses find a group that you're interested in marketing to.

3. Make a contribution to the current discussion *as a fellow small business owner.* Your signature line should be your only advertisement. Note, too, that many lists restrict the length of signature lines.

4. Participate in the e-mail list regularly and often, offering value but not blatant advertisement for your business. Participating in mailing lists is a subtle way of getting the word out about your business.

Alert the Media

Having a new or updated website is no longer big news. If you want to be interviewed or profiled by a major or even local news outlet, you must find a way to pique their interest. Examine your business and think of what is newsworthy. Can your business be tied into a story related to current events? Link your business with a particular holiday and offer something special enough to appear in the local section of your community's newspaper. Stage an event (host a political rally, arrange for a famous author to give a workshop), or conduct a survey

All business sectors should address the following items in their press release. The example statements are from a group of healthcare professionals who focus on helping patients with depression.

Define your product or service. "Our revolutionary therapy has helped patients suffering from chronic depression by stimulating the area of the brain responsible for happiness."

Point out how your product can benefit the public. "Happy people are productive people. Recent studies show that depression costs billions of dollars in lost productivity."

Talk about the unique aspects of your product. "Using patented technology, we stimulate specific nerves that in turn stimulate areas of the brain that control mood. Patients report having a more positive outlook and calmer thoughts. Our technology has proven more successful than the traditional pharmaceutical approach."

Find a compelling hook. "Winter is the peak time for seasonal affective disorder (SAD) and our therapy has proven to be a cure." "Our product is the ultimate in busting those holiday blues."

Spotlight customers or clients who are willing to be interviewed by the media. "Our company can provide the names of patients who are willing to talk about their depression and how our technology improved the quality of their lives."

The final step is to determine what media will reach your target audience. Send your press release to newspapers, magazines, radio stations, and television stations, and websites and blogs that cover news.

and notify the local media of your groundbreaking findings. Get involved with charity or volunteer work that helps your community.

Once you've written your press release send it via e-mail to whatever local, regional, or national media that caters to your target audience. You may want to use a web news service, such as PRWeb (www.prweb.com) and Xpress Press (www.xpresspress.com) to spread the word around the Internet.

Sample Press Release

The Women's Finance Institute (WFI), a group designed to help women get funding for their businesses, used a recently published study as the hook to promote their services. The group was able to provide a woman who could speak about the benefit of their services. Furthermore, WFI could help the city correct its poor record for women business owners.

For Immediate Release

Centerville Ranks below National and State Average for Women Business Owners

Centerville, Kansas, August 10, 2008: *Business may be booming in our city but why is the number of women business owners below both national and state levels? A survey on small business released earlier this month from the city's chamber of commerce and the Centerville Community College showed that only 17 percent of the city's business owners are women—compared to 28 percent nationally and 27 percent statewide.*

"There are a couple of reasons, but one of the most pressing is the lack of access to capital," said Jessica Strayhorn, vice president of the Women's Finance Institute.

Despite the bleak financial news, the tide is turning for women.

Meet April Bacon, president of an information technology firm. Bacon launched her business with the help of a microenterprise loan, which helped her buy her first Internet servers. "I never would have been able to start my own business without the Women's Finance Institute's help. Not only have we increased our staff to ten but I'm considering opening another branch."

TOOLS FOR WOMEN

As the leading provider of financial products for local women business owners, WFI offers access to

1. Microenterprise loans: Launched by a series of successful female entrepreneurs to give a hand up, not out.

2. Venture capital: Money that can help launch or sustain a business.

To set up an interview with April or the Women's Financial Institute, call 444-555-1212 or e-mail us at press@yourdomain.com.

ABOUT WOMEN'S FINANCIAL INSTITUTE

Founded by ten successful businesswomen whose goal is to help inspire and educate women to start and maintain businesses.

Website: www.yourdomain.com

TWELVE

FINDING THE TIME
TO DO IT ALL

Now that you are equipped with the tools you need to boost your business, the next step is creating a way to integrate all that you've learned into your business and your life.

When you started your business you probably created a business plan and a marketing plan to get your business off the ground. Now, to succeed at marketing your business on the Internet you need a new media marketing plan. But this is not a typical forty-page business/marketing plan filled with competitive analyses, industry trends, and balance sheets. It is not a dense plan or a vague road map or a complicated system; it's a simple, six-step, integrated approach to quickly take you down the path of new media success. It's the Ultimate New Media Blueprint that puts all you need to do in one handy plan. It all begins after you set up your website, e-zine, blog, and podcasts, as discussed in Parts Two through Five.

Ultimate New Media Blueprint

1. E-zine

Determine the themes for your e-zine for the next twelve months. Schedule time to write one themed article each month. The more articles you can write in advance, the more time you'll have later. Try writing all twelve articles in advance, or write three articles every quarter. As soon as an issue is complete, send it to your e-zine hosting service and set up the delivery date so it will be distributed to your subscribers.

2. Blog

Use your e-zine themes to create topics for your blog posts. Schedule time to write two short posts (two or three paragraphs) each week. If possible, write all eight posts for each month at once and then set them up for automatic, scheduled publication with your blog hosting service. Don't feel locked in by your themes or by having written your blog posts in advance. If something in the news will affect your customers or if you come up with a new product or service, you can either add an additional blog post or change one of the scheduled posts. Having eight to twelve posts in the queue takes the stress away and gives you the luxury to provide bonus material. Schedule some time each week to read and respond to any comments left on your blog.

3. Podcasts

Use your monthly themes and record or film at least one podcast a month. If possible, try for a semimonthly audio podcast schedule, or better, a weekly schedule. Like your e-zine and blog, try to prepare these episodes in advance and schedule them for release through your podcast hosting service or RSS feeder.

4. Optimize Your Website

Outsource this task or schedule time to perform basic maintenance on your website and be sure to change the "last updated" date. At a minimum, your website should be updated every time a new issue of your e-zine is published, whenever you post to your blog, and whenever you release a video or audio podcast. Any product or service mentioned in your other new media components should be featured on your home page. Be sure you change your article page often, and update your personal information whenever you win an award, earn a certification, or publish a book. Check that your website links and blogroll links are still current. If you run specials or sales, you need to set up a schedule for getting that information on your website.

5. Syndication and Distribution

As discussed throughout the book, your new media publications should be listed in directories, databases, and search engines. Make sure each new publication is properly tagged and distributed. Check that your RSS feed and other automatic distribution systems are working as they should. This can also be outsourced.

6. Get the Word Out

Continue to get the word out about your business. Schedule time to check out your social media pages and your e-mail lists and groups. Read and leave comments on the blogs of related businesses.

Making the Time for New Media

If you keep doing the same things—the same old way—you'll keep getting the same old results. It is now time you move your business to the next level of success.

New media marketing is the solution to accelerated communication with your prospects and customers. One of the biggest drawbacks of implementing any radical change to the way you have always done things is finding the time to do it!

Implementing any marketing strategy requires commitment, but the good news is that you're spending time on something that is the most relevant and efficient way to reach your target audience. The Ultimate New Media Blueprint helps you find the time to integrate all your new media components.

Like all important traditional marketing strategies and tactics, such as networking and speaking, you must schedule time for each task to gain effective results.

To begin, start with your calendar and the Ultimate New Media Blueprint. Decide what you will do weekly to market your business. Once you put something on the calendar, commit to treating it as you would any other important appointment. Be sure to block out enough time to do the task you need.

Some business owners may not have blocks of time to dedicate to their new media efforts. If you can't do these tasks during regular business hours, you still need to find some time in your weekly calendar. If it's not on your schedule, you're not going to do it.

A New Revolution in Small Business Marketing

It's a new frontier in marketing your small business where new media breaks down the barriers to communicating directly with your audience. Without a doubt, integrating new media into your marketing mix is a surefire way to propel your business to new heights.

You will reach masses of people in less time. You will say your messages in many different ways as you build and sustain your community of loyal customers. But it's not what you say so much as how you say it.

Marketing Blueprint Calendar

A management consultant who works from her home office has selected her themes for the next four months. Take a look at her calendar to see how she has successfully integrated tasks related to the Ultimate New Media Blueprint into her workweek.

Monday	Tuesday	Wednesday
7:00 a.m. Gym	7:00 a.m. Gym	7:00 a.m. Gym
8:00 a.m. Breakfast/shower	8:00 a.m. Breakfast/shower	8:00 a.m. Breakfast/shower
9:00 a.m. *Write & post blog entry/set up interview for tomorrow's podcast*	9:00 a.m. *Interview expert for podcast, post to iTunes*	9:00 a.m. *Write & post blog entry/ phone calls*
10:00 a.m. Client	11:00 a.m. Filing/check & respond to e-mails	10:00 a.m. Client
11:00 a.m. Invoice client/check & respond to e-mails	12:00 p.m. Lunch/industry reading	11:00 a.m. Invoice client/check & respond to e-mails
12:00 p.m. Lunch/industry reading	1:00 p.m. Client	12:00 p.m. Lunch/industry reading
1:00 p.m. Client	2:00 p.m. Phone calls/client work	1:00 p.m. Client
2:00 p.m. Phone calls/client work	3:00 p.m. Client	2:00 p.m. Phone calls/client work
3:00 p.m. Client	4:00 p.m. Check & respond to e-mails	3:00 p.m. Client
4:00 p.m. Check & respond to e-mails	6:00 p.m. Sign off	4:00 p.m. Check & respond to e-mails
6:00 p.m. Sign off		5:00 p.m. Sign off

Thursday	Friday
7:00 a.m. Gym	7:00 a.m. Gym
8:00 a.m. Breakfast/shower	8:00 a.m. Breakfast/shower
9:00 a.m. Chamber of Commerce breakfast	9:00 a.m. Client
10:00 a.m. Chamber Networking	10:00 a.m. Client
11:00 a.m. Stop in to see client	11:00 a.m. Invoice client/check & respond to e-mails
12:00 p.m. Check & respond to e-mails/phone calls	12:00 p.m. Lunch/industry reading
1:00 p.m. Client	1:00 p.m. *Write 1 e-zine article & set up for automatic delivery*
2:00 p.m. Client work	3:00 p.m. Check and respond to blog comments. Read and comment on other people's blogs. Read and respond to e-mail lists and groups.
3:00 p.m. Client	5:00 p.m. Sign off
4:00 p.m. Check & respond to e-mails	
5:00 p.m. Sign off	

As you can see from the management consultant's weekly calendar, it doesn't take a lot of effort to reap the benefits of new media marketing, once you've got your new media components in place. This consultant found a way to integrate her marketing tasks into the rest of her life and business.

Producing a typical podcast will take about an hour, once you get the hang of it, which you could do once per week. Each blog entry shouldn't take more than thirty minutes to write and post. Everyone can spare thirty minutes two times per week to get the word out about his or her business.

New media is the perfect medium to deliver your messages with truth.

New media allows you to offer value that makes a difference.

New media emphasizes your commitment to your customers.

Have fun with it all! Marketing with new media gives you the opportunity as a small business owner to express your creative self and enjoy your business and your life. You have come far since the beginning of this book. And where this book ends, your journey toward a more organic small business begins. We want to hear from you and may profile you and your business. E-mail us at successstories@newmediamavens.com. For monthly tips, guidance, and insights on how to improve your business's new media marketing, sign up for our e-zine at www.newmediamavens.com.

We wish you much success!

ENDNOTES

1. "Small Business Marketing: Use of Web Sites and Online Marketing Techniques," Jupiter Research, April 2007. Available online at www.jupiter research.com/bin/item.pl/research:concept/1209/id=99189. Accessed March 31, 2008.

2. "National Workplace Productivity Survey," Lexis Nexis, 2008. Available at www.lexisnexis.com/literature/pdfs/LexisNexis_Workplace_Productivity_ Survey_2_20_08.pdf. Accessed March 31, 2008.

3. Morkes, John, and Jakob Neilson. "Concise, SCANNABLE, and Objective: How to Write for the Web," 1997. Available at www.useit.com/papers/webwrit ing/writing.html. Accessed March 31, 2008.

4. Outing, Steve, and Laura Ruel. "The Best of Eyetrack III: What We Saw When We Looked Through Their Eyes," The Poynter Institute, 2007. Available at http://poynterextra.org/eyetrack2004/main.htm. Accessed March 31, 2008.

5. "2008 Annual Marketing and Media Survey Results," Datran Media Survey, 2008. Available at www.datranmediasurvey.com. Accessed March 31, 2008.

6. "JupiterResearch Finds Targeted Email Marketing Campaigns Can Generate Nine Times More Revenue Than Broadcast Mailings," Jupiter Media, 2008.

Available at www.jupitermedia.com/corporate/releases/05.08.16-newjupresearch .html. Accessed March 31, 2008.

7. "How Companies Can Enter and Remain in the Customer E-mail Inner Circle: A View from the Inbox," Merkle/Quris, September 2003. Available at www .qponmarketing.com/news/Email_Inner_Circle.pdf. Accessed March 31, 2008.

8. "Blogging Is Bringing New Voices to the Online World," Pew Internet and American Life Project, July 2006. Available at www.pewinternet.org/PPF/r/ 130/press_release.asp. Accessed March 31, 2008.

9. "The State of Blogging," Pew Internet and American Life Project, January 2005. Available at www.pewinternet.org/pdfs/PIP_blogging_data.pdf. Accessed March 31, 2008.

10. Verna, Paul, "Podcast Advertising: Seeking Riches in Niches," eMarketer, January 2008. Available at www.emarketer.com/Reports/All/Emarketer_ 2000474.aspx?src=report_head_info_sitesearch. Accessed March 31, 2008.

11. "Google Receives 64 Percent of All U.S. Searches in August 2007," Hitwise, August 2007. Available at www.hitwise.com/press-center/hitwiseHS2004/ ussearchenginesaugust20070920.php. Accessed March 31, 2008.

12. "Can Viral Video Clips Drive Targeted Traffic?" MarketingExperiments.com, November 2006. Available at www.marketingexperiments.com/improving-website-conversion/viral-video-clips-targeted-traffic.html. Accessed March 31, 2008.

13. "OfficeMax's ElfYourself.com Surges Past 75 Million Elves—Will It Reach 100 Million before Christmas?" OfficeMax, December 2007. Available at http://officemax.mediaroom.com/index.php/press_releases/434. Accessed March 31, 2008.

14. " 'Digital World: State of the Internet' Report Highlights Growth in Emerging

Internet Markets," comScore.com, March 2008. Available at www.comscore
.com/press/release.asp?press=2115. Accessed March 31, 2008.

15. "Blog, Podcast, RSS Advertising Grow Fastest among Alernative Media,
Surging 198% in 2005 and Forecast to Grow 145% in 2006," PQMedia.com,
April 2006. Available at www.pqmedia.com/about-press-20060411-amrs1
.html. Accessed March 31, 2008.

16. "The Strength of Internet Ties," Pew Internet and Family Life Project, January
2006. Available at www.pewinternet.org/pdfs/PIP_Internet_ties.pdf. Accessed
March 31, 2008.

17. "Younger Internet Users Are More Likely than Older Ones to...," New
Media Institute, January 2006. Available at www.newmedia.org/articles/14/
1/Younger-Internet-Users-are-More-Likely-Than-Older-Ones-to/Page1.html.
Accessed March 31, 2008.

18. " 'Digital World: State of the Internet' Report Highlights Growth in Emerging
Internet Markets," comScore.com, March 2008. Available at www.comscore
.com/press/release.asp?press=2115. Accessed March 31, 2008.

COPYRIGHTS AND PERMISSIONS

INDEX

ABOUT THE AUTHORS

Photo by Bobby Cochran/
www.bcphotodesign.com

Lena Claxton and **Alison Woo** are the principals of New Media Mavens (www.NewMediaMavens.com), a company that offers coaching, seminars, and solutions for small business owners.

Alison Woo (left) is a journalist with extensive experience in television, print, radio, and online media. She has worked for *CNN Headline News* and with Emmy Award–winning anchor Linda Ellerbee; she has worked as a freelance writer for national news organizations, including FortuneSmallBusiness .com and MSNBC.com. An alumnus of Columbia University's graduate school of journalism, Alison was an executive producer and writer for television stations in New York City, Tampa, Sarasota, Orlando, Charlotte, and Atlanta. She was a contributing writer for *The Weekend Entrepreneur* and *Women's Wire Web Directory*. Alison is currently a member of the International Coaching Federation and has trained at the Coaches Training Institute, the leading coaching organization in the United States. She is also a member of eWomen Network and the National Association of Women Business Owners (NAWBO).

Lena Claxton (right) has extensive marketing experience helping entrepreneurs and authors market themselves on the Internet. Before joining New Media Mavens, she was marketing product manager at Baker & Taylor, Inc., the world's largest book distributor. Lena is an online and offline marketing instructor with Central Piedmont Community College's entrepreneurial division. Her syndicated articles on marketing have appeared on websites around the world. She is a graduate of Rutgers University and University of Phoenix, with a graduate degree in online education. Lena is currently a member of the International Coaching Federation and has trained at the Coaches Training Institute. She is also a member of eWomen Network and the National Association of Women Business Owners (NAWBO).

For more information on marketing with new media, visit www.New MediaMavens.com.